Plethora:
Ancient Techniques and Advanced Technologies
for Creating a Wealth Consciousness Within
- An Esoteric Guide w/ Application Techs and Tools –

By

William H. Mayweather

Plethora:

Ancient Techniques and Advanced Technologies for Creating

a Wealth Consciousness Within

- An Esoteric Guide w/ Application Techs and Tools –

First Published 2012

Copyright © William H. Mayweather 2012

Golden Mean Publishing

ISBN-13: 978-0615642215

ISBN-10: 0615642217

Dedication

This book is dedicated to my children who have yet to be conceived, my powerful daughter Ananda and my extraordinarily intuitive son, Shekem. I also dedicate this work to all who have and will traverse the depths of their imagination with the goal of manifesting their optimal existence and uncovering their true life's purpose(s).

Contents

Why I Wrote This Book

Quite simply, because I couldn't find what I needed in other books on the subject. I needed that which would be a condensed esoteric manual and quick-guide for developing two of the most important facets of my life, spiritual and financial well-being. Long have I looked for information on wealth creation written with an esoteric basis/foundation.

Writing this book has been a labor of love; primarily for myself and secondly for those who have shared in my dissatisfaction over the mounds of authors who write about wealth consciousness but only from a surface level; never diving into the depths of the matter to release the core concepts to the populace.

My own personal spiritual journeys lead me to prefer techniques that offer accelerated progress in return for my dedication. I read about the monks in Tibet that are dedicated to a life of meditation and inner unfoldment. Also the sadhus in India who live a seemingly nomadic life of meditation, while depending on God for every form of sustenance. "Is this the life for me?" I had to ask myself. Born and raised in the Bronx, NYC, I could not deny that my mind was bred on western ideas of life, love and spirituality yet I had a longing for the beauty that I saw within eastern ideals.

Once I realized that there seemed to be two worlds influencing my life, I had a choice to make. Would I mold my ideals based on my environment and my upbringing (in which I had no say so in the matter). Or would I use the spiritual concepts of the East to direct me in all my endeavors. I had to be completely realistic. I simply could not imagine sitting in a cave or a temple in the heights of the Himalayas meditating without ceasing. I also knew that many of the ego-centered ways of life sanctioned by western society would not sit well with my soul. A deal had to be struck. I felt an undeniable need to serve my fellow human and I also craved for the boons given to those who are dedicated to spiritual evolution.

I wanted my cake and to eat it too; I mean it only makes sense, right? I remembered watching Bruce Lee movies, wanting to be him. I remember reading about spiritual aspirants in the east that could defy certain laws of nature and perform some insane feats of mental and physical prowess. I also remember wanting to help feed families and provide much needed financial support to those in need. I wanted to be the type of person that would take the shirt off his back to clothe someone else. But that would take money, so I understood its importance.

It was time to truly begin to understand who I was. I noticed that I had an aversion to "meditation". Instead of that, I decided to work on sustaining a waking trance state that would keep me in a centered and spirit-filled state, but this was outside of the general view of what "meditation" was. After seriously questioning my thoughts and actions, I realized that I simply had no patience for conventional meditation and spiritual practices which usually entailed emptying the mind for a prescribed amount of time (usually years) and bending my body into elaborate postures.

I also believed that there were better things to do with trance (a byproduct of meditation) than just clearing the mind. So I never meditated (in the conventional sense). I wanted shortcuts. I feel most people need shortcuts in this day and age of smug, car emissions, tainted foods, neurotic people, unscrupulous leadership, etc. It is unrealistic for most to sit in a lotus position for 50 years to intuit the nature of the universe.

Subconsciously, I made a wish. I asked for ways to traverse my mind in less time than what was considered "normal". Eventually, I was given what I asked for. I was given ways to "cheat". If walking is the conventional way of getting places, then hopping into a car would be considered an unfair advantage. Spirit/God/The Big Wig in the Sky (and in my chest) lead me to ancient and modern technologies that offer insight into the human super-computer (the human mind) and to core spiritual concepts.

Combine these two forces (ancient and modern technologies) and you get a celestial gift. I am here as only a messenger presenting the gift of the ages - the gift of spiritual achievement, financial gain and true, unadulterated happiness by way of advanced techniques and technologies.

SECTION I: THE KEYS TO THE CASTLE (THEORY)

CHAPTER 1:

What is Wealth Consciousness?

What a provocative subject responsible for mounds of thought and almost as much misunderstanding. To truly even have a chance of getting a beneficial definition, and by beneficial I mean one that can be of maximum use, it is suggested, that you NOT take merely an outside external view or train of thought. Don't look through your physical eyes which are trained to see and define the outside world. Look with your inner eye and scan the depths of your soul. Only then will you enter the chasm of the knowable.

Before the major discourse begins, let us briefly discuss the word "Life". Life/Living is associated with two fundamental factors.

1. First, it is the ability to achieve what you want, in the inner AND outer worlds (Balance).
2. Second, it is getting stuck/ensnared in either the inner OR outer world (Imbalance).

About "worlds"... we live in two worlds, simultaneously. The inner is the intimate world of the unconscious where our decisions are made, where our plans are devised and where the different parts of us battle for ultimate supremacy (if not in balance). I should bold, italic and triple the font of the words within the parenthesis of that last sentence. The question of balance is of ultimate importance.

When imbalance exists, the world becomes a land of fog....Where you can't see the forest for the trees. Complication lives within this imbalance and clarity is simply non-existent. This unbalanced life leads to getting stuck (either in the inner world or outer) and getting UNstuck proves to be a job for champions. Well friend, after reading this book you will become a champion....A master of your own universe.

Take a moment to consider how life and wealth relate. Life and wealth are closely related like first cousins. Or better yet, brother and sister twins.....identical - from the same egg.

Wealth is an expression of life. In fact, it's the ultimate expression of life. Wealth can be equated to the life energy that you **express**. It's nothing more than an extension of your life-force. To create wealth a person must have a mental set up that is drenched in expression and freedom (as opposed to the self-imposed imprisonment that most people call their lives).

If you do not have wealth, no one can be blamed but you. You are just not expressing the life energy within you towards wealth. Everyone wants wealth but very few actually increase the life energy within them that corresponds to the level of wealth that they say they want.

The usual/normal view held by many so-called spiritual people is that renunciation should be taught and should be the focus. But think about this. How can you renounce unless you have lived? A rich man can take part in renunciation. A poor man can also take part in renunciation. Are they equal qualitatively? No. Wealth in and of itself is not bad. As a matter of fact, it's good. Wealth's origin resides in creation, wielded by those who are in cahoots with the supreme creator (many times without their conscious knowledge).

Wealth As An Expression of YOU

To properly discuss wealth, it is necessary to move beyond looking at it as just a physical phenomenon (more on this later). If you don't already agree, you soon will agree that wealth is in the being and not so much in the doing.

When a man/woman with a correct understanding about wealth decides to create wealth, he will attract that which he wants and he will have a great fulfillment caused by living a greater expression of himself. All his energy will be focused on creating and not destroying. Notice this. Those interested in destroying others or inflicting some sort of violence towards others are completely dull; they don't shine. They are dead in their very consciousness. Those who work towards creating wealth are working towards unfoldment (on some level).

Creating automatically makes a person non-violent because the whole of their energy is directed towards creation. They are too busy creating to worry about inflicting pain on others. Therefore, creating wealth brings about a tremendous interest in life; non-violence being a byproduct.

As we are aware, creation begins within the human spirit and it manifests in the outside world. Creating wealth is godly, if you're contributing something directly to people or to the universe. Only those methods borne of dishonesty are wrong; they are not true wealth creation at all. True wealth can be celebrated and no ill feeling should crop up within the doer or any other party involved. Creating wealth is an intrinsic part of life AND living. Why? One – you are creating. And Two – wealth is an expression of life.

There are rich men that carry a deep guilt imposed on them by society even though they created their wealth very honestly and creatively.

Because of the guilt imposed on them, they live a very miserable life. There are those who drink heavily and take massive amounts of drugs in an attempt to try to forget this guilt.

The fact of the matter is that they should not imbibe the guilt given by the people who are incapable of achieving. As long as they did not lie, cheat or steal to get their wealth, there is no need to carry guilt around (like a poodle named Fufu in a Louis Vuitton handbag). Yet and still, many rich people carry this guilt very deeply, in their core. Just to escape from it, they get into all kinds of addictions. To those types reading these words at this very moment ….. I ABSOLVE YOU NOW. Now get the heck outta here.

EVERYONE'S first priority should be enlightenment. Until that happens, the second priority can be creating wealth…but not by robbing or stealing but by creating. Anything else is a third priority which we will not be discussing. The prerequisite process goes as follows.

1. First, you must remove any guilt that you carry about wealth. It should be purged from your inner being.
2. Second, understand that the wealth you create is equal to your expression of life. So the more and more life energy you express, the more and more you will be creating. Life energy expression and Wealth are one and the same (as seen through our inner eye).

Debilitating Wealth Concepts vs. Proper Wealth Mentalities

Most of our intimate beliefs about wealth are completely flawed. Our incorrect thought patterns about wealth normally waver between three skewed concepts. If you don't have wealth, you have a fear of loss; possibly hording what little you have. If you do have wealth, you have a

level of greed resulting in not using what you have for its greatest good.
If you are in between the two, you harbor worry, anxiety and lack
security.

For many, the moment the word wealth is spoken, past failures stream
into the forefront of their minds. They remember past "mistakes" which
awakens much pain and suffering. "Normal" folks seem to put the
accumulation of wealth as their first priority but, in truth, most cannot
think of wealth in a relaxed fashion.

Know that if you are confused about wealth, you are confused about
You. Who you are. What you are. Why you are here. The more you
attain and cultivate oneness (throughout your being), the more wealth
will miraculously gather around you. Without the right mental set up
about yourself, you are in store for an uphill climb, up the steepest
slope from which bodies can be seen on the rocks below.

Wrong ideas about wealth become a self-impediment to personal
growth, abundant living and an understanding of our true nature.
Proper thinking (about wealth) not only attracts it towards you but it
adds incredible clarity to your day-to-day life and activities.

It can't be overstated, how important it is to first clear out all the
wrong/incorrect concepts about wealth. This is even something that
should be done prior to proceeding much further in this book.
Otherwise you will not be able to see the inner workings of creation and
its byproduct, wealth. If wealth is only seen as a concept that exists
outside of the human spirit, it will be nearly impossible to attain and
sustain

CHAPTER 2:

The Lame Excuse Formula:
Work NOT Done + Valid Excuse = Work Done/Finished

Now, it's time to talk about secret desires. The only reason they are secret is because they go ignored and suppressed. The term "Keeping it Real" comes to mind. Oh yes….that trite term used to death in a faddy sort of way. Keep it real? What are they really talking about? They're talking about the ability to admit the truth. First to ourselves. Then to everyone else (maybe). So what does wealth have to do with keeping it real? As humans, we validify our decisions. We find ways to justify not only action but inaction.

There are people out there, probably the masses, who have a desire to have large amounts of money. They don't have it though and that's absolutely fine. The problem lies in our justifications. Humans are ego based beings, who often place other people's opinions in the forefront of their minds. This effects a person's actions and can cause them considerable anguish when they do not stack up to other people's opinions on how and who they should be.

Whenever they feel that they won't be accepted because of an action (or lack of action), they go on justifying in a way that is not completely in line with truth. This is a huge weakness that must be conquered. Only then can a person get closer to living the fullness of what life has to offer.

When wealth is the subject, instead of honestly admitting why we are where we are (which is often painful), we paint a splendid picture. The picture depicts a bigger person who is fully in control, but this is usually not the case. The real picture would be possibly of an ant amongst giants. Even admitting our insecurities brings us to the heights of unfoldment and evolution.

I tell you the whole thing is backwards. Admit the unflattering parts of yourself and you will slowly be released from them. There is a Hindu belief that says that whatever we speak from our mouths, will be burned in the fire of sacrifice. Those were layman's terms right there, by the way. Speak your truth constantly and be constantly refreshed.

Ever heard of this one, Keep it 100? There is some sort of intrinsic understanding out there that truth comes in degrees. Keep it 100 means to tell the truth….the whole truth and nothing but the truth. It means to keep it 100% real. Even in their truth, most people lie and they do it subtly through erroneous justification sprinkled with a little bit of truth (which is more dangerous than a blatant lie).

Below is the formula used, by the masses of people, concerning wealth.

They have a desire for wealth. But they don't have wealth. Now they begin giving valid (but not necessarily truthful) reasons for why they don't have what they say they want. Of course, they do this with countless other subjects but we're discussing wealth here. Correlate this to other subjects and realize that we justify all over the place.

The Lame Excuse Formula (LEF) goes something like this:

Work Not Done + a Valid Reason = Work Done/Finished.

There is no striving within this lie. The mind is so cunning that it creates very valid reasons (for our actions or inactions) and then it justifies itself. It gets diabolical. For example, there are those that have not been courageous and gone for their dreams or their optimal life. They are poor but not just on the outside; they are also poor internally. This poor man state of mind becomes their station in life.

Soon they begin adding sacredness to their poverty. What they are really doing is adding sacredness to their scaredness. They are fearful. Because they are scared of life (they lack the audacity to live fully), they back away from living. They are actually scared yet they justify the fear by adding sacredness to it.

They come up with bone-headed excuses like "Oh no, I'm not the type that can tell lies and I am not the kind who can cheat others." Or "oh, I just need a little to live ... one small house and a couple of pieces of clothing – that's enough for me."

IF IT'S ENOUGH, WHY ARE YOU GOING AROUND BRAGGING ABOUT IT? I use the word "bragging" to make it clear to you that they are using words (which they pour from their ego) to cause a feeling within those they are "bragging" to. They usually want to elicit some sort of feeling within the other person so that they will be accepted or so that their point of view will receive some invisible stamp of approval.

You can tell they are not content because they keep talking about it (whatever it is). If they were at ease, they would not even speak on it so much. To the trained eye, they give themselves away every time. The fellows who talk about their poverty being a great quality will not keep quiet about it because they're trying to make sacredness out of it. They're trying to convince you and themselves. Very Cunning!

People brag about their wealth to try and create an identity from it. People also brag about their poverty and try to create an identity. At least when people brag about wealth and try to make an identity out of it, they are just a little more intelligent (than the poor braggadocios fellows) because they are in creation mode (unlike the sacred loin cloth wearer). Bragging about poverty and creating an identity from it is even more damaging to your system than bragging about having. Brag about being poor and stagnation will persist.

Keeping it Real releases. Tell the truth. Try it and notice the heart feeling. It's lighter. Let your body be the gauge.

Spiritual seekers often justify their poverty as their spiritual quality of innocence or something. If you have decided not to create wealth, then GREAT. Conversely, if you have greed for wealth or a strong desire for wealth, you are not really a spiritual seeker. It's all in your priorities.

Enlightenment should be the first priority. A person can have a problem with not having wealth. A person can have a problem with having wealth. Both are problems. Both are sicknesses. If you suffer from either, go internal with honesty and courage and you will resolve your issue. Just be persistent.

A word of caution: In your journey towards life-force expression/wealth, you will find that most of the problems you'll face in your life will come from the people who are poor and who try to add sacredness to poverty. This is very immature. Rich people, often times, are more mature and are more sincere when they take up spiritual paths in their lives. You may also feel the opposite side of the above. You may experience pressure by those who have "attained" on some level. They may stir within you a feeling of inadequacy. By prepared for both and protect your mind from any disempowering opinions.

The same way that stealing and accumulating wealth in the wrong way is a sin, not creating is also a SIN. It normally means that you are not singing your heart's song. You are not realizing your divine purpose. You are locking up your light inside your chest. You are not expressing, your actions are probably not focused and you are not being responsible. A good motto to follow is "be true to your-self, if no one else". Know what you are doing in your positive and negative actions/thoughts. We all have dualities. Know what you are being when you are being it.

Like the old 80's G.I. JOE cartoon slogan … "knowing is half the battle."

Below are some examples of the Lame (Ass) Excuse Formula in action.

The Formula:

Work NOT Done + Valid Reason = Work Done/Finished/There is Nothing More to do.

The Formula in Real-time:

Lose Weight + Family History of Obesity = I Will Not Make a Real Effort
Ignoring Bills + "I Don't Make Enough $ to Pay Them" = I Have No Bills (this will catch up to you fast)
Financial Instability + "I Only Make $10 an hour" = Can't Help Myself or Anyone Else

Don't cultivate this type of thinking. There is, always, work to be done. Keep It Real w/ Self. Keep it 100.

CHAPTER 3:

Death by a Deep Hatred for Work - A "Wasted" Life

[handwritten note: ↓ word power. : trabajo ↖ work in spanish]

Many of us have mental blockages and an extreme aversion to work. It's necessary to push past this and change our relationship to work. Life's flow is work. What would life be without work? You may already know. You may be experiencing the chaos of broken duties and a slothful existence. Are you happy with that? Is it fulfilling? Are you content? I highly doubt it.

There is an interesting concept that just came to mind. I vaguely recall reading it in some book several years ago. It talked about how work and worship are synonymous. It discussed how a person's work should be their worship and that this erroneous ideal of separating the two, has caused un-fulfillment across the planet.

Let's look at a job for a minute. Usually, people spend between 8 to 10 hours a day at a job, 5 times a week, 50 weeks per year. Notice: this is more time than you spend with your families/loved ones. We often separate our jobs from our real lives but I'm here to assert that your job is an extension of your life whether you'd like to admit it or not.

So, time for the hard questions. What are you doing for work? Is it a celebration of who you are? Do you put on a mask when going to work? Is your "work" in line with your ideals? Is your "work" your worship? Should it be? I won't answer these questions for you but I think you catch my drift.

As you can see, there are different kinds of work. There is the work that you don't do (that you know you should) and there is the other kind – that which you do to make a living. Are you making a living or slowly dying inside? Wake up calls are sometimes abrupt.

Now …. Back to wealth! If you are not creating wealth, all your work is happening in the wrong direction. Your work is happening more in the line of destruction not creation AND it could be termed self-destruction. Does what you do bring you fulfillment or does it bring you anguish OR do you play the escapism game? Be honest with yourself; it's the road to greater happiness.

Even the loss of money can prove to be a huge benefit as assets can also come in the form of lessons learned. The lessons you learn become more valuable than the situations that try to affect you. There are no mistakes so live and learn but know that time is not infinite. Waste too much time and you may find yourself on your death bed haunted by regret. Remove your deep hatred for work. Life is by its very nature, flow. Flow is movement. Move towards a greater expression of your life-force.

If you create wealth, at least you will be directed towards creativity. If you are not creating wealth, you will be spending all your time destroying something or somebody (most likely yourself) or you will be spending all your time fighting something (like depression). Know that ultimately, you are fighting with your Self (capitol "S").

Check out this grand battle:

- In the morning you urge yourself to get off your fake-royal behind and do something to create wealth and a happier life.
- The evening comes and you say, "You know what? ... maybe tomorrow."
- The next morning comes and you say to yourself, I should really be doing something to create wealth or to change my life.
- In the evening you will argue, no no, I won't create now because I have something better to do (your favorite reality TV show may be on).
- At night you fall asleep.
- Between morning and evening, you will be spending time eating, daydreaming, defecating, spending time with family and friends, on and on and on but that's all. This cycle seems endless to most, but it's not endless because we all eventually die.

After 20 years, what have you done? "I debated in the morning, whether to create wealth or not (on the side of creating in the morning). In the evening, I debated for not creating wealth. Finally, nothing has happened. Life is wasted. Awaken the creativity in you and remove your hatred for work/creativity.

To be creative (to create), you must be willing to accept many new responsibilities and toiling [working very hard] may be necessary. Find that which excites you then be ready to work. Your excitement, passion and courage will carry you through. None of this is easy. Would you even appreciate it if it were? Take responsibility. It doesn't happen like a breeze but even if the breeze comes, you have to be responsible enough to keep the doors open - for the breeze to flow through you.

CHAPTER 4:

The 3 Dimensions of Wealth

The 1st Dimension - Creation and Enthusiasm

The creation of wealth can be boiled down to one word....intense high enthusiasm. OK ... that's three words but the operative word here is Enthusiasm. Radiate high enthusiasm in anything you touch; in everything you do. If you collect garbage, maintain high enthusiasm when doing it. If you dig ditches, maintain high enthusiasm. WHATEVER it is .... Maintain high enthusiasm. ⟵ MAXIMUM EFFORT

Maintain high enthusiasm for 11 hours per day for 21 days. Give it a try. NO, give it a DO. Do it as a practice. Do everything in this manner and you will not only attract wealth to yourself but suddenly your very attitude and life will take a quantum leap forward. High enthusiasm is wealth. If you radiate high enthusiasm in whatever you do, you'll wind up making that particular activity a sacred activity.

The spiritual aspirant knows that fulfilling his/her being is much more important than fulfilling his/her desires. Fulfilling your desires is such a small task in comparison. A true master fulfills his/her being. Enthusiasm can never be brought in from an outside source, but must be brought out from within. It's an internal quality, like breathing.

Enthusiasm (or lack thereof) can be a gauge of your quality of life. Enthusiasm is joy overflowing through your intelligence.

You cannot use anything outside of yourself to create enthusiasm; for it is a force that emanates from within. Enthusiasm and addiction are completely opposite from each other. Things which addict you can never give you enthusiasm. Things that give you enthusiasm can never addict you. Please don't think that you can create enthusiasm through alcohol or drugs. It just doesn't happen. Maybe dynamic excitement can result but is not enthusiasm. In dynamic excitement, you are not creative. You are violent and/or destructive. With enthusiasm you are not dynamic or excited. You are only enthusiastic. Whenever you are filled with enthusiasm, you are experiencing God intensely in your inner space.

High enthusiasm is real wealth and an experience of God. All other things (even if they are called wealth) are fleeting. Extraordinary enthusiasm is the basis for creating wealth. The extraordinary, reasonless enthusiasm is awakened only by inner practices and that is why you are reading this book. Knowing the internal practices will offer you a shortcut by cutting through the external to the core concepts – the nitty-gritty.

Creating wealth without enthusiasm creates a corrupt wealth which cannot be maintained/sustained. Wealth is something that a person should be able to celebrate, if nothing else, but internally. The lightness of being should exude from you. Enthusiasm is an inner quality that has to be awakened by awakening your life-force. This is a gradual process (short-cuts to follow) that will culminate in more and more wealth due to more and more expression.

When life-force is awakening, wealth becomes a by-product. There is an old Sanskrit saying that when Kundalini is awakened, wealth becomes your servant. Kundalini is life-force energy. In order for wealth to be your servant, you'll need to become wealthy in your very consciousness. When high enthusiasm is awakened, wealth gathers around you, stays around you and you will maintain stability if it leaves you.

The greatness of wealth and it's flow is that it can leave you. Understand that when it leaves, it teaches a lot more lessons than when it comes to you. If you can maintain high enthusiasm when wealth leaves you, you'll learn some extremely valuable lessons that raise you to a higher level than when wealth originally gathered around you. It may leave you under a good circumstance or a bad circumstance; either way, be prepared, maintain your enthusiasm and you'll turn out even more powerful than before.

The 2nd Dimension - Sustenance and Maintenance

Sustenance/Maintenance wavers between two poles: Holding (i.e. a treasury) and Circulating (i.e. currency = moving like a current). When holding, accumulation happens. And you accumulate …. And you accumulate …. Never enjoying it and not letting others enjoy it either. There is not necessarily any knowledge of why it is accumulating. No one knows what is going to be done with it. It is there for the future….Some "rainy day". When is the future going to come? No one knows. This is normally wealth accumulated out of insecurity. Understand that wealth will never be useful when you are really in need. When you are in need you think … "no, no, no, a worst need will come so I'll keep it for a bigger emergency."

Sounds like fear to me. Feels like fear to the doer. Being safe is rational and you should be rational but never touch the extreme side of this. If you do, you may cultivate a hoarding type of energy which will deplete you of any enjoyment you could have had. Be aware.

Now circulating wealth is a whole different concept all together. Another word for money is currency, which has its root in the word Current. Current is defined as a flowing; flow, as a river or something that flows like a stream. They don't mention accumulates like a pond which can get pretty murky. Circulating wealth means to constantly share it and get satisfaction from it. All this is very similar to a child with a toy. The purpose of a toy is to play and play and play and share but often times it is coveted. Have you ever seen a stingy kid? It can turn the most precious being into a selfish tyrant with a poked out lip.

The 3rd Dimension - Money Leaves You - Go Bye Bye?

OK….let's say wealth leaves you. It packs its bags and decides to go. If you follow the above suggestions, you will come out on top and wealth will be banging down your door again. Survival is all in the cultivation of the life-force and living an enthusiastic life. Remember this.

CHAPTER 5:

Rewiring Your Brain for Success

Let's bring in a different way of thinking for a minute. A different way of looking at reality, if you will. Can a person ever truly fail? I mean, what is failure? What is success even? Who are you? Are you the totality of who you present yourself to be? Are you mainly your conscious thoughts and actions? Are you mainly your hopes or your fears? Are you mainly your conscious mind or your subconscious mind? I'll leave you to think about the answers to those questions as it relates to you, but I think you see what I'm getting at.

Your subconscious mind is the generator of your experiences, and, no matter what we say we are, the subconscious mind is there to either support our claims or call us a liar. I propose that we are mainly our subconscious minds. Assuming that the former statement makes complete sense AND assuming that our subconscious mind is the generator of our experiences, do we ever really get what we don't want? Well, Yes and No. Consciously, we do not get all we want but on a subconscious level, we absolutely do get all we want. Subconsciously, we cannot fail. Subconsciously, we are a rousing success, all of the time.

If you are not successful in your life, you worked for failure; so, failure is your success. Put another way, if you are not consciously successful in your life, you worked for failure on a subconscious level thereby making you a success based on the directings of your subconscious mind.

At the opening of this book, I mentioned the importance of looking at ideas and happenings with your inner eye as opposed to your two physical eyes. Your inner eye can place its gaze at the inner workings of the cosmos and yourself, thereby opening the door to the understanding of the relationship between the larger macrocosm and your personal microcosm.

Embracing the above concept again lets you know that the power is within you, has always been within you, and has always been working to bring into reality the seeds existing within your subconscious mind. But know that the problem may be in the seeds that have been planted. You are not necessarily responsible for planting all your seeds but at some point you will need to take responsibility for the seeds you allow to flourish. Insecurities are seeds. Fears are seeds. Love is also a seed. Compassion and caring are seeds too. Cultivate those seeds that empower you. Till the soil of your mind and your heart.

The goal is in the alignment; the alignment of conscious and subconscious forces within you so that they work in unison. Note that the subconscious mind will ultimately be the victor in all occasions. You want success, don't you? Do you want your subconscious mind on your team working with you? Or do you want to continue to do battle with yourself? Do you want full-fledged success in all facets of your life? Alignment is Key; success is a side effect.

There are Three Layers/Levels of Success:

1.   What society calls success = Your Work
2.   What spirit calls success = Your Worship and Spiritual Practices
3.   What the individual calls success = Your Life (combines the above)

The above levels of success seem to be separate but in fact this is an illusion played by the differentiating mind. Looking at the three as removed from one another produces a discontent within your system. All three should be in sync and become one full expression of Life.

It is possible for all three to be aligned so that one doesn't contradict the others. These days it seems almost natural to have this wrong concept that spiritual pursuits, financial success and societal success should conflict. They are not meant to conflict.

There are so many misconceptions about how an individual sees success, how society views success and what spiritual success is and how it feels. The ultimate definition of success as per the individual is the spontaneous fulfillment of any need happening within your inner space. These days, what we think we need is completely warped. Materialistic greed has us in eternal conflict; wanting all the money and the power but not understanding that our purpose and what resonates within, has a simpler path leading to even more fulfillment.

Your true need is only based on the seed you have within. An acorn seed produces an oak tree. It does not produce an apple tree. An apple seed does not have the ambition to produce a pear tree. If you are unconscious in thought, will you have the need beyond the seed that you carry. If not careful, greed can overtake your personality making you insatiable with an unending yearning. All conscious and aware beings carry the need only based on the seed they have within. Your need should be based on the seed you are carrying.

There are those who want Bill Gates money and there is not anything necessarily wrong with this but you should know the seed you carry and the need it creates. What may be a better pursuit is to work towards the fulfillment of any need that arises. Know yourself and face your supposed failures. Don't be self-sympathetic and don't justify your weaknesses. Simply (but not so simply), face your failures and know that you are a success if nothing more than on a subconscious level. Then go visit your subconscious mind, consciously and duke or hash it out.

There is no need to lie to yourself and no need to hide. You should allow the truth to attack your inner space and wreak havoc, if necessary. At least you will be able to rebuild and move towards true and complete fulfillment and not just the supposed success that we call our fragmented, one-sided triumphs and victories. Rewire your brain for all three levels/layers of success. Rewire your brain to not justify ignorance and laziness.

There is no real scale for individual and spiritual success, so naturally we build theories based on our conditionings and agreements in life. We often times turn these theories into attitudes we hold about life but really they are a buffer to avoid looking at, and feeling, the failure we continue to cultivate.

We stagnate ourselves because of our own weaknesses and inability to honor our minds and hearts and their demands. You want something that your mind introduces as an important need, yet you can't or won't bend for or yield to some of the things your mind demands.

I.e., you work a job that you hate. You are unappreciated, over utilized and you live paycheck to paycheck. You know you should do something else. At least, find a place where you can be you and not have to mask your true identity. You know this but what do you do? You remain where you are. You don't make a change. You dedicate your one life to being smaller than you actually are or less than you can be. Is this by choice? :) Lack of discipline, a bad relationship with time and the idea of boredom all contribute to our folly, but our main issues exist within the psyche.

CHAPTER 6:

The Problem of Fragmentation Within the Psyche

Inner fragmentation is the primary ingredient required for internal strife, struggles with others and a lack of effectiveness when working towards your goals. It is something that we all should be working to annihilate but before we tackle the problem of inner fragmentation and how it affects wealth (creation), I believe it necessary to briefly discuss the concept of archetypes.

As the word itself implies, archetypes are related to types. They are types of character traits or a set of qualities that seem to appear over and over again in recognizable patterns. Psychological archetypes are patterns that form the basic blueprint for the major components of the human personality. These are compulsive personality traits that affect everything that we do. They are inborn; we all come with a set. Each of us has a great multitude of distinct personalities co-existing within one body, sharing one psyche.

An archetype is a force that can seize you ….. take you over without your conscious consent.

For instance, love at first sight. Many don't even believe in the idea of love at first sight but let me explain what happens in these supposed cases. You have an image of yourself – unbeknownst to you – as a woman (if you're a man). Now you see that woman (or a good imitation of your "type") and instantly, you are mentally taken away to the land of mush. You have turned into mush at the sight of your archetypical counterpart. Afterwards you may discover that it was a huge mistake. The intelligent man believes that that woman was chosen by him but if he really ponders the event, he will realize that he has been captured (and maybe tortured;). He had no choice in the matter.

Another example is fury. Fury just sounds uncontrollable. Something happens and the anger is so concentrated that a person can lose all rational sense.

In this same manner, any concentrated feeling can overtake a person. Archetypes are these feelings (or forces) personified in their most extreme state. We all are a hodge-podge of these personas or archetypes. We are erroneously lead to believe that we are a singular personality but we're actually a conglomerate of energies and forces and sometimes these forces are in disagreement/disarray. They struggle within us causing a battle between our conscious wants and our unconscious demands. This is a maaajor problem.

Active Imagination is a powerful technique to promote oneness within (see section II, chapter 3). Understand that the forces within you need to be on the same page in order for any goal to be realized and sustained.

Let's say that you consciously want to acquire wealth. You think you want it with all your being but your unconscious mind gets in the way. The little girl inside (an archetype of you) may be fearful of the new world that will open up for you. Or the creative artistic old man within may fear that he will be "killed" if you persist in analytical and focused thought. Know that if these forces within are suppressed or not given what's due them, they will cause internal strife; and the ultimate battle rages on. This is a problem for the majority of people out there who "attempt" to attain their idea of wealth.

Inner work is the key to opening up a dialogue between the conscious and unconscious aspects of the psyche. Inner work helps bring inner conflict to the surface where they can be dealt with. The conflicts are there whether we chose to face them or not and can involve urges, values, beliefs, morals and ways of life.

Most people are unable to face inner conflict. They impose a kind of artificial unity on life by clinging to the prejudices of their ego and repressing the voices of the unconscious. Many people believe they can achieve their goals by going backwards, avoiding the conflicts and pretending they are not there. We can't go backwards and retreating is NOT an option.

Inner work shows us that we can embrace the conflict and courageously place ourselves in the midst of the warring voices and find our way through them to unity. Balance only comes when all of our sides are given their due. The warring parts of ourselves can be brought together into a peaceful union. This alignment is necessary when it comes to creating wealth, sustaining wealth, being able to enjoy wealth AND allowing others to benefit not only from our wealth but also from who we truly are inside.

CHAPTER 7:

Mental Programming:
Reprograming the Super Computer Called (INSERT YOUR NAME HERE)

Your Mind is a Battlefield

So …. how long has it been since you've been trying to overcome some personal obstacle? Whether it be smoking, drinking, losing weight or making money. Each day we're bombarded with ways to supposedly fix these problems but few of them actually work because the source of those problems lies deep within our own minds …. the subconscious mind to be exact.

Our subconscious mind holds the key to our health, wealth and happiness. People spend thousands of dollars per year on personal development courses that just don't work in the long run. We use these personal development products and they may work for a while but most of us end up doing a U-turn, finding ourselves right back where we started. Your subconscious mind can be your best saboteur. You may be in for the fight of your life, if you don't have the proper tools. In comes Mind Programming.

The basic goal of Mind Programming is to change one's reaction to internal and external stimuli. It can also be used to help your mind create a physical or emotional effect on its own (i.e. confidence or happiness). Mind Programming incorporates a number of theories and techniques used to harness the brain's built-in programming mechanisms to help end bad habits, stop negative mental patterns, help enhance intelligence and so much more.

All of our minds are programmed and that's a fact. Have you ever hopped into your car and suddenly arrived at your destination without knowing how you got there? I mean, you know you drove but you just don't recall the details. Have you ever driven past a fast food restaurant and immediately felt stomach pangs (although you may have recently eaten or may even be on a diet)? Both of these are a direct result of mental programming and conditioning. I'll offer you some powerful techniques in this book.

Deliberate Mind Programming has existed for thousands of years. Yogis have used deep meditation for mind programming. Hypnotists have been programming the minds of people for over one hundred years. Huge advancements have been made and today people can use carefully prepared audio and visual stimulation to induce a variety of mental states most of which leave the mind more receptive to reprogramming.

You can make your subconscious your ally; training it to respond correctly to situations that may arise. You can also change your life, surroundings and circumstances because the subconscious mind actually paints the picture of your past, present and future experiences. Keep reading and you'll find out how to access those powers in order to change any area of your life (see section II, chapter 5).

Mental Programming and Hyper-Suggestibility

A Mental Program is a set of instructions embedded deep inside of the human brain. Based on some internal or external stimuli, the mind and body leap into action to follow the set of instructions previously given to it. Mental Programs are normally subconscious thereby out of our conscious control. One reason is that many Mental Programs are coded during traumatic experiences. Another reason is that Mental Programs are often state based; meaning that they can only be remembered in the same state as to the one in which the program was first coded into memory.

Most mental patterns are formed during the first 7 years of our lives and are influenced by the words and actions of our parents or guardians. During the first 7 to 8 years of our lives, our brains are functioning mostly in the Theta and Delta brainwave state (more on this to follow). During these years, our minds are in what is called a hyper-suggestible state and are prone to accept statements as fact when they are coming from an authoritative figure.

For example, there is a little girl, 6 years of age who is singing and loving life while doing it. A parent may be incorrectly dealing with the normal stresses of life and inadvertently shouts to his/her daughter "Shut up and Be quiet, you sound horrible". Trauma!! That little girl has most likely just developed a complex. She may never sing again. Or a parent may become frustrated with a child when they are having difficulty reading, possibly hitting the child and saying, "You'll Never Learn". The child's mind, being in a receptive state, would associate the act (reading) with the negative experience (getting hit). The parent's statements or actions can perhaps lead the child into learning problems and self-sabotaging behavior later on in life.

There is always hope (even years and years later). Mental Programs can also be intentionally programmed or coded into memory. With some of the tactics in this book, people can reprogram their minds, erasing old unwanted programs and adding new healthier programs to the subconscious mind. This can be done by stimulating brainwaves to create specific mental states bringing us to a point of hyper-suggestibility. The science works both ways. Be very excited.

Hyper-Suggestibility is a term that describes a state of consciousness where information is rapidly absorbed into the subconscious (bypassing the normal mental filters). It's a state of extreme receptivity to suggestions and images. While in this state, suggestions are much more likely to be accepted and acted upon. Look at a very young child for the greatest example of hyper-suggestibility.

All would agree that children learn faster than adults but few ask why.

The main reason is because children spend the majority of their time with Theta and Delta being the dominant brainwave state. While in this state, kids don't' only learn how to spell, do arithmetic and say NO. They also learn how to survive, relate to the world and how to think. This is the time that the subconscious is being formatted.

Let's look at the example of driving, one more time. Little Bobby or Emily is 16 years old now and they are badgering their parents to teach them how to drive. As a matter of fact, think back to when you were learning to drive. At first, you may have been very nervous, having to constantly watch the road (like a hawk, even). I used to squint even though I wore glasses, myself. Conversations were very distracting because all of my concentration had to be focused on driving. Eventually I learned how to drive and so did you. Now you can drive to work and back and not even remember the experience. This is because driving has become a subconscious activity and thought is no longer required.

Similar to when a guy sees a pretty girl and uses some cornball line on her; she has already developed a premade script to shut him down. Even greater than this, your subconscious has developed an action to suit almost every situations. If you don't like public speaking, it's because your subconscious mind has built up a nervous reaction to it. If you like something, it is because your subconscious has developed a good reaction to it. Most of the time you'll have no idea where these mental programs are coming from, because they were coded into memory while you were a kid; at a time when your subconscious was growing faster than your long-term memory.

Hyper-suggestibility happens mainly in the Theta brainwave state (where children spend most of their time). In the Theta state, learning things and committing them to the subconscious is fast and furious. But in "adulthood", you only enter the Theta state while sleeping or when using mental tools and techniques. Modern technology has made this very easy to reprogram or deprogram ourselves.

A study was done by Felipe at Yale University where attitude-changing affirmations were given to subjects during various mental states. Only during drowsiness or sleep did the affirmations have any significant effect. During alert, waking states and deeper sleep stages, the affirmations had little to no effect on attitude and behavior. Today, there are devices and computer programs that assist in bringing a person to the theta brainwave state. In fact, these tools can take you to theta, gamma, alpha and back to beta (see section II, chapter 5).

Understanding brainwave patterns and how to manipulate them can prove extremely valuable when it comes to developing a wealth consciousness. The fact of the matter is that many of us (or most of us) have programming within our subconscious minds that cripple our ability to achieve our goals. Something within us undermines our actions and causes us to live in a loop of sorts - spinning our wheels, if you will. Mental Programming/Reprogramming should definitely be a consideration. Modern technology allows us access to the deep recesses of our minds where we can restructure our brains for our highest good.

CHAPTER 8:

Willpower vs. Imagination – NOT a Fair Contest

Use your willpower to get what you want, they tell you. Use your willpower to force changes in your life. If you can't stop eating unhealthy foods or if you can't stop smoking, for instance, then your willpower is weak. Do not heed this type of advice given by well-meaning people who are usually trying to "help". I'm here to tell you that your willpower is not where your true power lies.

Your willpower is designed to fail you. Willpower is a tool born out of the need for a mental function that will allow us to bypass our own programmed mental orders. But let me ask you, which is more powerful, your mental commands (associated with willpower) or your mental programming? Well, it depends.

Some of our mental programming is so deeply rooted in our subconscious minds, that willpower is simply not enough to allow us to circumvent these subconscious demands. For instance, have you ever tried to relax when you were extremely upset? The more you tried, the more you failed. Or, if you're a guy and you're having sex, have you ever tried to stop an orgasm by willing it NOT to happen? You know that all this does is make it happen even quicker, but, if you start thinking about power tools or mowing the lawn or some other non-sexual subject, you can usually stop orgasm before it happens. By the same token, the person that is extremely agitated would have greater success imagining something pleasant rather than just willing him or herself to be in a better mood.

This speaks volumes. The true power resides in your Imagination. You've heard the term "I'll believe it when I see it". This is precisely how the subconscious mind works. What the subconscious mind sees, it believes. That's why a guy can be so close to the point of orgasm and then stop it by placing his mind or mental attention into another place, doing another thing.

I feel the need to say it again. What the mind sees (or is made to see), is what it believes. Do you see how much power and control you actually have over your life? You are not a leaf blowing in the wind. You can glide and go where you wish.

What about this saying: "perfect practice makes perfect". Most people believe that just "practice makes perfect" but the truth is that "perfect practice makes perfect". Let's talk about it.

Here's an experiment for you. Get a sheet of paper and ball it up. Make a spherical throwing device...a ball. Get a garbage can/trash can and position it on the other side of the room that you're in. From the other side of the room, shoot the ball into the garbage as if a basketball and a hoop. Do this 10 times with your eyes **open** and focused; and do try to make it. Next, **stop**. Now **close** your eyes and see yourself shooting the ball and getting it into the basket perfectly each and every time. Do this 10 times. Now, **open** your eyes and shoot the ball 10 times again (eyes open). Notice – that your stats go up....waaaaay up.

When you're experiencing something (in your mind), your subconscious mind let's down its guard and accepts what it is seeing as true. The subconscious mind cannot tell the difference between imagination and real experience. Don't take my word for it. Test it for yourself. Or just think back to all the times you drove past McDonalds and got hungry instantly. Your mouth just watered when you laid your eyes on those golden arches. Your body has been trained to react. You know you're not even hungry but just the thought of the fries, the way they smell, made your body respond, made your stomach growl, made you salivate … all activated by your imagination.

With the use of sensitive medical equipment, scientists can see the parts of the brain that "spark up" when a person has an experience. What's astounding is that precisely the same areas ignite when the person is asked to only imagine the same experience. The neurological electrical response is identical whether the action is really happening or just being imagined.

What does all this mean? It means that your imagination can be leveraged for your benefit. Imagine yourself healthy, and your mind, thinking it is real, will act to make your visualization a reality. The subconscious movement towards the change happens on a very subtle level. For instance, if you imagine yourself healthy and strong, your body may begin to burn calories a little faster or you may begin getting a strong urge to exercise or eat certain healthier foods. This subtle level is not limited to you or your life but it affects the realities of other people's lives as universal intelligence begins to work for you, through you and others.

SECTION II: ADVANCED TECHNIQUES THAT CATAPULT (PRACTICE)

CHAPTER 1:

AWAKENING THE DRAGON WITHIN

MEDITATION EXERCISE TO STIR YOUR INTERNAL GATE-KEEPER

Manifesting Ideas into Reality (Thought)

Do you remember floating in your mom's womb? Probably not, but think about the sheer power involved in the process. You came into being from certain energies that were in your mother's womb. You were conceived and that began the gathering of all that was necessary to make you, you. That seed energy manifested your physical body and it still exists within you. Now what if you knew how to *consciously* place an idea into that source energy?

We all place ideas into source energy all the time. We are continuously manifesting but unfortunately we normally manifest on an unconscious level, which is why we are unhappy and dissatisfied. There is the best kind of hope in these statements. We all have the capacity to consciously place an idea into source energy and make that idea a reality.

The power of manifestation can be wielded any way you see fit. Any situation that manifests can be completely changed; the trick is in knowing the science of conscious manifestation. Many of the problems in our lives derive from our unconscious manifestations. Even now, most of us are unconsciously manifesting our future turmoil. It need not be this way.

Conscious manifestation means doing exactly what you want to do and achieving what you want to achieve. Any idea that you want to quickly make a reality should be taken to the level of the kundalini (the life-force). The life-force within you is responsible for the manifestation of your body and your mind. When you take the seed/idea to the life-force energy level, any idea you sow quickly becomes a reality.

Manifestation is the science of consciously altering reality and experiencing reality as you see fit. Our energy system, the body, is not to be overlooked as we are the conduit or the projector. Before we fully venture into the advanced techniques, it is advised that we use exercises and breathing techniques with the goal of purifying and cleansing the body's energy channels. I will briefly describe a practice that was developed by illuminated sages in India prior to the Dark Ages. It's called Kriya.

WHAT IS Kriya? (Practice)

Kriya (in Sanskrit "action, deed, effort") most commonly refers to a "completed action", technique or practice within a yoga discipline meant to achieve a specific result. Types of Kriya may vary widely between different schools of yoga. Another meaning of Kriya is the outward physical manifestations of awakened Kundalini/Life-force. Kriyas can also be the spontaneous movements resulting from the awakening of Kundalini/Life-force energy. -------------------- Definition courtesy of Wikipedia

Kriya is a technique that intensely awakens your life-force and manifests whatever seed form existing within your inner space.

The Steps:

- Step 1: Cleaning the nostrils. Inhale deeply … then … exhale deeply. One inhalation followed by one exhalation is one cycle. Do this 11 times or for 11 cycles.
- Step 2: Pull lower abdomen in and up and breathe. This will feel like you're first flexing your lower abdomen and then your upper abdomen. Do this 21 times.
- Step 3: Inhale as slowly as possible, fill your lungs and hold as long as possible. Exhale as slow as possible and hold your lungs empty as long as possible. Do this 21 times.

The first three steps are just preparation.

- Step 4: Stopping the senses. Place your thumbs on your ears. Place your index finger and middle finger on the eyes. Place your ring fingers on your nostrils. Place your pinky fingers on your lips. Lock all the senses including your nostrils. Stop the breath. This step should not be done if you have high blood pressure or any other heart conditions. If you have any serious illnesses, don't do this step. Just sit in silence and meditate. All others are fine. Lock down all the senses and turn your attention to the energy inside you. You will notice a subtle stirring within your being. This is the stirring of your life-force energy which will grow based on your vigor or consistency. Hold all the senses as long as you can and when you feel that you can't hold them anymore, relax the nostrils. Inhale deeply and exhale deeply. Your body will balance itself. When you feel balanced, again hold your nostrils, and ears and eyes all over again. Do this 21 times.
- Step 5: Intense humming for 7 minutes. This is for preparing the body for a more intense kundalini/life-force

awakening. Humming has the effect of balancing and
settling the energy within you.

- Step 6: Become an open channel between the sky and the
  earth. With this step it is necessary to mentally feel a union
  with all that is around you. Use your imagination to develop
  a mental connection with source energy. When you are
  filled, pour yourself onto the ground (in your imagination).
  Be an open channel between the sky and the earth. Use
  your imagination to maximize the practice. Do this 7 times
  or for 7 cycles.

- Step 7: Sit for just a few minutes and feel intensely
  connected to source energy. Send a deep, loving, blissful
  vibration to the whole world. In this moment, you will feel
  subtle changes in your body as your kundalini awakens and
  enthusiasm rises.

This is a brief introduction to a sacred secret that is not available to the
general public. This ancient technique, called Kriya, is very powerful and
is known to greatly benefit your mitochondrial cell energy and activate
the deeper strands of DNA. Practice with care and patience.

CHAPTER 2:

Sexual Transmutation

Sex Magic

Sex Magic is a term used to describe the process of tapping into source energy, using sex, and directing it via willpower. A premise of sex magic is the concept that sexual energy is a potent force that can be harnessed to transcend one's normally perceived reality. One practice involves using the energy of sexual arousal or orgasm with the visualization of a desired result.

Transmuting sexual energy comes down to bringing the energy from the genitals up and through the body. It means taking sexual sensation, the feelings that are in your genitals, and bringing them up through the entire body. It's consciously bringing the sexual energy up and dispersing it throughout your body.

Doing this invites a whole other greater power that can be used for manifestation of creativity or whatever it is you want. Sexual energy is the most powerful energy in the world. So all the sensations you feel in your genitals derive from the most powerful energy there is….sexual energy. Imagine distributing this energy throughout your entire body and your whole body being awakened and NOT just your genitallia.

You can transmute sexual energy through your breath, through laughter, even through crying. Emotion is the key. Like a York Peppermint Patty – Feel the Sensation. OK....i couldn't resist.

Ways to Sexualize Your Brain

Sexualizing your brains means taking all your sex energy and injecting it into your consciousness. Every neuron of your brain needs to be infused or bathed in the emotional energy of sex. There is extreme value in taking all of your sex energy and directing it towards a noble purpose, such as creating wealth.

It's all about taking the desire of sex or the feeling of wanting to have sex or wanting someone (whether your spouse or someone on TV or a neighbor, whomever) and using that energy for a purpose besides orgasm. It's like watching your spouse getting out of the shower; glistening and looking good ... It's got you going. You take that feeling and keep it but you change your thought; focus it on wealth or health or whatever your particular goal is.

Now, you don't have to have a spouse to take up these practices (although with sex magic w/ a partner, I would suggest you practice with someone you have a deep connection with....more on that in the next chapter). You don't really even need a physical partner. You do need someone to stir these sorts of energies within you; the stirring takes place in the mind. It can be anyone. The "who" is not important. It's the feeling that's important.

You need to take that feeling of being aroused and excited and you change the thought from sex to prospering whatever it is that you're trying to do. Whether it's growing a business, getting a promotion, becoming healthier, you take the feeling and infuse it into a new thought.

Remember that thought without directed action has little power even if the thought is riddled with emotion. It's important to take the thought and add an action to it; such as starting a business.

Feeling + Thought + Action = Fruition

Put forth effort, cultivate Enthusiasm and Focus Your Energies.

The process of taking the desire to have sex and transmuting it results in that good feeling (what better way is there to describe it)...that confident feeling. So when you're going out, and putting in that application for that new job, you are feeling good and therefore letting off good feelings and vibes (short for vibrations). When you sit down for the interview, you are giving off a powerful feeling that is subconsciously being recognized by the other person or people.

The trick is using your memory to dive into this aroused state.

Try this test for fun. Go into your bathroom and look into the mirror. Just a normal look. OK...notice how your face looks. Notice the contours and the subtleties of your expression. Remember how you look. Now turn around with your back facing the mirror. While your back is to the mirror, get yourself into that aroused state by remembering a sexual experience you may have had or by imagining someone that you are sexually attracted to. Now turn around and face the mirror again. Look into your own eyes. Notice the subtleties again. You have a different face. No, it's the same face but there is something different. Something more attractive. Something more alluring. Something more powerful. There you see it. You can use this. But Be Nice.

Sex Magic (With Your Partner)

Procedure:

- Take the time to prepare your ritual space. I suggest that the place or area where the ritual will take place be clean. Also, before you start your ritual, take a shower or bath and while doing so, visualize the water washing away all the emotional stresses that you've had throughout your life or throughout the day. Visualize all those emotional stresses being washed away. Before intercourse of any kind, you and your partner should sit down in front of each other, holding hands and synchronize your breathing. Inhale when your partner exhales and vice versa. Think about what you guys are trying to accomplish; discuss it.

- If you like, you can decorate your environment with candles, incense, flowers, things that are sacred to you. Use things that your soul tells you are right for the ritual. It could be a picture or whatever. Let your soul be the guide. Whatever you use, be focused on it. Your soul and your subconscious do respond to symbols.

- Protection may be necessary and I don't mean a prophylactic. Realize that sex magic is a very serious thing and you can bring in negative energy if you are not careful. While you are having sex, you do not want any energetic interferences. To thwart any negative interferences, I suggest imagining a huge white sphere covering you and your partner, for protection. White light represents pure positive energy in a concentrated form. This is why you see spiritual figures surrounded by white light or with a halo over the head.

- You and your partner should have a conversation about whatever it is you are trying to obtain and visualize it. This really could be anything. From wealth to health to a new job to a new home. It can be material things - whatever you need and want – Visualize it. I also suggest you visualize yourself getting a higher level of understanding from the spirit realm in order to benefit your soul and your partner's soul. You can visualize healing as well; whether it be for a loved one that is sick or a loved one that needs help or yourself, of course. You can even do this for people you don't know or even for the world in general. There are people suffering all over so at some point, help others by using these techniques. Let us not be totally selfish in our pursuits.

- During this ritual, I do recommend you speak out the affirmation words, which simply means to speak the words related to what you want to attain. This should be done during the act of sex. Technically, you do not even need to speak verbally. You don't have to say anything. You can silently say it in your mind. Even a more powerful idea is to imagine the symbols that correspond to what you want. This gets the most powerful force within you involved - your subconscious mind.

- A word of caution. You really need to take up this practice with someone that you have a soul connection with. If you pick a random person off the street or you practice with someone that you really don't know, this technique will not be as effective. It is all about vibration and how souls vibrate together. There should be a soul connection between you and your partner. If you can get "under the skin" of your partner, then there is power there.

- Enhancements: One thing you can do, as a powerful enhancement, is have the female goddess dance tantrically in front of the male god/husband/partner while he's sitting down.

The goddess should dance erotically and beautifully to get the god aroused, keeping eyes locked on one another at all times. How both parties view one another is extremely important. The more love and respect, the better. I used the terms god and goddess b/c it's a great way to acknowledge the power within each of us and to show reverence.

- The difficulty that may arise is in focusing, which is supremely important. Because of the excitement involved, it is very easy to get off-track and forget the thing you are trying to obtain. It is pretty hard to stay focused when you're having sex anyway. Practice will make perfect and I doubt you will mind practicing. It's important for both parties to know what they're trying to obtain and to stay focused on the goal during the sex act.

- Nearing Climax – you've reached the height of arousal. You and your partner are in tune. You guys are focused. Your hearts beat as one. You and your partner, both hold the thought in consciousness of the thing you are trying to achieve, the goal; you hold it during the orgasm. After ejaculation, the thought should still be held in the forefronts of your minds, as your heart rates slow and gently goes back to normal. If you follow these instructions, if you and your mate have a soul connection, and you stay focused, you will be using the most powerful forces in the universe - sexual energy and the subconscious mind.

- Halting the Male Ejaculation – there is a huge benefit to not releasing or climaxing but this technique is pretty difficult. It's not to be overdone, either. The process consists of halting all sexual activity just before the point of ejaculation and sending the seed which has traveled down from the brain, back up to the brain by use of your imagination. Before ejaculation, the male must stop and imagine his semen traveling back up to his brain thereby electrically charging his neurons. The process can be repeated 3 to 4 times during the act of sex. This tactic will get you what I call "the Glow".

This has been a brief explanation of certain tactics that can be used to stir the energy inside you and direct them towards your will. All procedures should be handled with caution and it is suggested that slow progression be the goal. Do not rush through in the hopes of faster results. The likelihood is that you will do more damage than good.

CHAPTER 3:

Active Imagination –
Repairing the Relationship with Your Selves

Active Imagination is a verb describing a dialogue between the different parts of a human being. These different parts of you live in your unconscious mind and because they reside in your unconscious, they seldom are given any constructive expression. This eventually leads to inner conflicts of all sorts. Active Imagination allows you to go into the imagination and allow the images to rise up out of your unconscious. In your imagination, you begin to talk to these images and interact with them. And they answer back.

You'll be shocked to find that they express drastically different viewpoints from those of your conscious mind. They express thoughts that you don't recall consciously thinking and they tell you things that you never consciously knew.

The essence of Active Imagination is your conscious participation in the imaginative experience. It's active because the ego actually goes into the inner world, walks and talks, confronts and argues, makes friends with or fights with the personas it finds there. You engage the other characters in conversation, exchanging points of view and eventually learning from one another. This quality makes Active Imagination different from ordinary daydreaming where you're merely watching the stream of fantasy that goes on in the back of your mind. Daydreaming or Fantasizing is like watching a movie in the mind, as opposed to actively participating in the stream of events that play out. The difference is in the conscious participation.

In passive fantasy you do not actively participate; you don't reflect on what is happening and you don't take an independent position relevant to what's going on. Most fantasies repeat themselves over and over again. Problems don't get resolved; the fantasy just plays and replays in our minds without it evolving into anything of benefit.

A great example is the phenomenon of worry. Worry is a form of passive fantasy that is experienced by all people at one time or another. Worry plagues some of us and can have debilitating consequences. As long as we remain passive and let the worry fantasy possess us, there is never a resolution. With Active Imagination it's possible to go to the worry, enter into dialogue with it, actively confront it to find out who or what the conflict is within us, and do something about it.

The Key to Active Imagination is to be active within your imagination; you must participate with your feelings and emotions. What you do in Active Imagination is a symbolic experience but it is still a real experience when your feelings and emotions are involved. This is a powerful tool for realignment of the different aspects of the individual.

Because you are actively participating, you end up converting what would have been an unconscious passive fantasy into a very conscious and powerful act of imagination. When done correctly, Active Imagination constructively gives you access to the voices inside your head; it brings the different parts of you together that have been fragmented, helping to resolve inner conflict. It brings about peace and cooperation between your ego mind and your unconscious mind. Wholeness is the goal, here, and entering into communication with the inner self can resolve inner conflict and create a unified front within.

The Four Golden Rules of Active Imagination

There are four rules that must be adhered to when venturing into Active Imagination:

1. Rule # 1 has to do with taking the proper precautions. It is better to be safe than sorry. Before starting Active Imagination be sure that there is someone available for you to call in case you become overwhelmed by your imagination and can't shut it off. This won't be an issue for most but there are people who delve into the realm of the imagination and fantasy and they can't find their way back to the "real" world. These types should have a partner/watcher when diving into conscious active imagination.

2. Next, Clear Your Mind. When you clear your mind of thoughts, you are opening the way for images to appear in your field of consciousness; you are preparing yourself to receive. **Whatever comes – Receive It.** Once you start judging and editing and second guessing, you end the process before it can truly begin. Just let it happen. Block the editor of your thoughts out and receive what comes.

3. Once it's there, keep an eye on it. **Whatever comes, follow it**. Something will show up. Once whatever image makes its grand appearance, it will become animated. Not like a Bugs Bunny cartoon. Animated meaning that it will start to express itself in some form or fashion. It may move around. It may speak. A bird may fly overhead in your imagination. A lone cloud may move across the sky. A dog may appear. Your dog from when you were 6 years old may appear. This is where the psyche is

beginning to show itself. This is the place where you should engage and converse.

4.   The 4th Golden Rule is more of a warning than anything else. There is a real danger of losing touch with reality and letting your inner work spill over into your outer world. As a precaution, you should never recreate places from your memory and never use images of people that you actually know. Always imagine new places. Make sure that the projections that come out of your mind are not of people that you regularly interact with. If you do, you run the danger of mistaking the inner world for the outer and a melee can ensue. Only use small details like a street lamp or a phone booth. Never imagine entire areas because building a world, in your imagination, from your memory is the easiest way to lose your grasp on what's real and what you've built in your mind. On a deeper level, know that you can affect other people with the work that you do in your own imagination. I won't go into this idea in length. It is better to be safe than sorry. Don't fantasize about people that you actually know because they are affected even if only on a subconscious level. Remember, the subconscious mind is the generator of our outer experiences.

If you do the above with some discipline and consistency, you will eventually have interactions with different parts of yourself. If you keep this up for, let's say, 30 days you will have a set of characters that are relatively stable. After 20 or 30 days of doing this in a disciplined fashion, you'll have a stable environment or place you can go to do your inner work. You'll have a set of characters; People you can talk to to get advice or feedback.

You can also take your dreams into Active Imagination and talk to the characters there. You can discuss your troubles or problems or your hopes and fears. There is much that can be done within your imagination and the benefits can affect all facets of your life.

It is of utmost importance that you create a real dialogue. Sounds crazy, but it is one of the healthiest things a person can do. Talk to yourself. When people take up this sort of activity, they may feel that they are faking it and that's a valid feeling. The key is to try and shut off the Ego. This is not daydreaming, although daydreaming can be the set off for Active Imagination.

When an image presents itself, just wait. You will know you are having success when the image (person or even thing) says something that you do not expect. Know that what is said may bewilder or shock you. It's when the dialogue does not come out of your Ego (or conscious mind), that you'll know you are having success and that someone/thing is speaking to you. Then it begins.

A Step-by-Step Approach to Active Imagination

In this section, I am going to briefly describe the approach that should be taken when venturing into Active Imagination. We'll briefly look at the things needed to begin your work, such as privacy, where you'll be doing this work, how you're going to record what comes through, and how to lock in the benefits of this type of work. We'll then take a look at the four stages of Active Imagination.

Recording What Comes Through:

- Pen and a Pad – you can record the events that take place in the mind simply by writing them down. The key is being able to quickly record what happens. I'd advise changing the case of the letters based on who is speaking. For instance, when your conscious mind is speaking, you can use upper case lettering. When your guest (whatever comes forth) is speaking, you can use lower case letters. You can also use abbreviations to better manage the writing. For instance, when speaking as your conscious mind, you can add the letter E (short for Ego) to the left margin of the page. When your "guest" is speaking, you can give it initials such as WO (short for wise old man).

- Using a typewriter – works while for those proficient at typing. I'd suggest using the same tactic above of changing your letter case and use initials to note when you are speaking, in your imagination, and when your visitor is speaking.

- Using a recording device – this is probably the best tactic as you can verbally record what happens and then write it down later. Remember, the key is to quickly record what happens; and you want to record as much as you possibly can.

- Special Modes of Recording – there are people that have a special talent for an art. Such as dancing, painting, drawing, sculpting, etc. (the dancing reminds me of the movie Sucker Punch which is a wonderful example of Active Imagination). If dancing, grab a camera and record the movements. Whether painting, dancing, sculpting or whatever, it is still a good idea to write down at least some of the events that take place.

The Setting – Where It All Goes Down

- It is of utmost importance that you decide on a time where you can be alone. You cannot have an appropriate dialogue with your inner self if there are constant interruptions from kids, pets, doorbells or any distractions whatsoever. Set aside at least 30 minutes for each Active Imagination session (although 1 hour is suggested when brand new to the procedure). In the beginning, you may have trouble with the invitation but with time, something or someone will present itself.

- You must also set aside a room where you will not be disturbed. There should be no distractions. You should be alone so that your Ego won't get the best of you. When other people are around, humans tend to customize their actions and their speech. If other people are around, it is likely that you will become embarrassed and modify your actions. Take the phenomenon of singing in the shower. This is a time we can let our hearts out and sing because we are alone and away from the judging ears of others. Find a place where you can be free to shout, dance, whatever you feel you need to do.

The Four Stages of Active Imagination

Step 1: The Invitation

The first step in Active Imagination is to invite the creatures of the unconscious to come to the surface to make an appearance; to make contact. We do this by removing our attention from the external world and placing it into the imagination. Empty the ego-mind, direct your inner eye (attention) to a place inside then wait to see who comes to play.

To invite doesn't mean to manage. If you are trying to manage what happens during Active Imagination, you are sabotaging yourself before you even begin. You must learn to allow. All in all you're clearing the mind of thoughts of the external world and then you just wait with an alert and attentive attitude to see who or what will appear.

Many people get stuck on the clear your mind part, as shutting down your thoughts is not always an easy task. Those who meditate know how difficult it was in the beginning to "simply" stop thinking. This tactic requires great patience and concentration but, there are alternatives.

Alternative #1: Fantasies

You can use your fantasies to jump start your active imagination. In its simplest form, you look at the fantasies that have been running through your mind and you choose an image, a situation or a person. Then you go to that place and that person and use it as a starting point for Active Imagination. Participate in the fantasy, enter into dialogue with the characters, record what is done and said thereby converting this passive fantasy into authentic Active Imagination.

When you have a recurring fantasy that stays in your mind all day, it indicates that there is some inner problem that needs to be worked on. This technique is perfect for handling issues that barge into your mind in the form of passive fantasy (i.e. worry). Instead of letting the fantasy repeat itself wastefully, you bring it to the consciousness and actively work on it. We are taking "self-help" to a whole new level.

Alternative #2: Places

You can also visit places in your mind that are symbolic to you. For instance, you can place your consciousness into your childhood home and start exploring to see who shows up. This is very much like "going to your special place". Your special/inner place may be your childhood home, or a garden or a prison cell or a moonlit beach. Find the place inside you where the energy is strong. Going to your special/inner place is another great way to start Active Imagination.

Alternative #3: Personification

And yet another way to start Active Imagination is by using
personification. You can make your invitation by personifying a feeling.
This is a way to get warmed up. If you have a mood that you can't
shake, you have a strong hint as to where you should go to start your
dialogue with the unconscious. Go to the one inside that is depressed,
obsessed or in a foul mood. Go to it in your imagination and say: "Who
is the one inside me who is depressed today? Where are you? What do
you look like? Please take some form I can see and come and talk to me.
I want to know who you are and what you want." Remember, accept
what or who comes and converse with it. Don't judge.

Alternative #4: Extend a Dream

Another way to make an invitation is to use Active Imagination to
extend a dream that has gone unresolved. One goes back into a dream
(in imagination) and enters into a dialogue with the characters there.
This technique allows you to continue the story, go through the next
step the dream is leading you towards, and then resolve the whole
issue, entirely.

So when you want to do Active Imagination but can't seem to get
started, you can use any of the above methods to jump start you on
your journey.

Step 2: The Dialogue

Images begin to rise into your consciousness. They have accepted your invitation and now you are ready to begin a dialogue. In this dialogue you must let the inner figures have a life and voice of their own. You must also give yourself over to your imagination and just let it flow. I suggest you be candid during the discourse with your inner self. Ask what the persona wants. What they want you to do. Don't be controlling. You must show a willingness to listen.

When the inner figure does something, respond but be attentive. It's fine to ask questions. In fact, it's recommended. The inner figure may ask you to do something. You are free to say No and give reasons why. An inner character may try to lead you off your path. You don't have to go anywhere you don't want or do anything you don't want. Follow your heart yet don't be afraid of being uncomfortable.

The more you express your feelings, the easier it will be to begin a dialogue. By expressing yourself, you give permission to your inner figure to do the same. You can get an exchange going by letting it out. Whether it is - what you're afraid of, what you love, what you desire, what you feel about a situation, express it. This may lead to a heated discussion of the conflict between this inner persona and what you think you want (or don't want), or what you are afraid of or disapprove of.

Remember to write down what is happening and what is said. Writing helps you stay focused on your goal and it keeps your mind from wandering off into an unconscious fantasyland. Handwriting, in particular, helps etch the experience more vividly into your mind.

A One-on-One Conversation w/ an Aspect of Self:

Once you start a dialogue with an image that has risen out of the unconscious, it is important to not allow yourself to be distracted by other fantasy material that may come into your mind.

Stick with the image that has presented itself, start a dialogue with it and stay with the situation until there is some kind of resolution. If you allow your mind to drift, you will find yourself in a meaningless loop of images and situations.

Active Imagination should consist of a statement of a problem, an interaction with the differing views and opinions and then a resolution to the issue/conflict.

Participate with Feeling:

Complete participation is a requirement. Although the action is happening on the inside, one must sense that what is happening is real. Be present within your feelings and express them. When you know that what is happening is real and you participate with feeling, an onlooker (and there should be none) would be able to see any physical reactions to fury, hurt, disappointment, loathing and joy, happiness, gratitude, etc.

A word of precaution against control and domination: You must not try to determine what will happen, what will be said or what the outcome is going to be. Exerting this level of control will stop the free flow of thought and expression. Try not to dominate the conversations. Give all parts involved equal time to express their viewpoints.

The same rules of courtesy, tolerance and respect that exist in the outside world, exist on the inside world. Don't try to make the inner figures sound intelligent or customize anything about them. Let them be what they are. Do not make a discussion on what message should be coming out of the situation. You are not yet at that stage.

Your only objective here is to express your feelings and to record what happens or what is said.

Listen More Than Anything Else:

Our conflict is normally with the parts of ourselves that have been relegated to the shadows. They may have been suppressed by our ego minds and kept out of conscious thought. These are the ignored parts of ourselves that we have dishonored or kept mute. You may find that they have unpleasant things to tell you and they may be upset that you have been seeing them as inferior parts of your personality.

It is your turn to listen. A part of your unconscious may call you a tyrant or it may have some choice words for you. You must lovingly listen to this under-expressed part of yourself.

For once, you must listen to that "inferior" being as though he or she were the voice of wisdom. Know that your depressions and weaknesses may come to the surface too. You must empower yourself. Speak lovingly to yourself. Realign yourself. Honor all parts of yourself.

The dialogue may not always be in words. Sometimes the entire experience takes place through action....through seeing and doing. You must still be listening.

How to Reply:

When first learning to honor the voices of the unconscious, there is a tendency to go overboard. People mistakenly lean towards the idea that the unconscious is all-knowing and the ego becomes the jailed prisoner. This approach is as off-centered and as unbalanced as the egotistical approach.

The goal should be the harmonious unification of values and ideals, within your being. Your unconscious mind can become your biggest ally or your worst enemy.

In the same way that the ego needs to go to the unconscious to balance itself, the unconscious needs to be balanced by the viewpoints of the ego. The goal is a win-win situation. The conscious mind has a duty to engage the unconscious in discussions and actions aimed at creating a synthesis of ideals.

Manipulation is Not Allowed:

Active Imagination should remain in the realm of the unexpected. It is extremely important not to manipulate what happens during Active Imagination. Don't go in with any prepared scripts. You may know what you are looking for when you go into Active Imagination. You may know what you want to say. You may know how you feel about something. But do not think that you know how the inner persona is going to react or what the inner persona is going to say. You won't know until it is said.

You have the right to say whatever you want but you do not have the right to plan what they're going to say and you don't have the right to dominate them once they appear. You should go about these steps without controlling or manipulating anything that flows out of the unconscious.

The system of Active Imagination is not to be confused with hybrid systems that came out of the Law of Attraction phenomenon; where it became the in-thing to use the imagination to get what you "want". The values attached to these other systems (born in the western hemisphere) are not supportive of the ultimate goal of Enlightenment. Where Enlightenment should be the primary and most important goal (followed by wealth/creation); wealth has become the primary objective and Enlightenment follows as a close 2nd, or 3rd or not at all.

The main difference between Active Imagination and these other systems is that everything is predetermined in these "modernized" versions. The ego decides in advance what is going to happen in the imagination and it prepares a script.

The general idea is to "program" the unconscious so that it will do what the ego wants. Guided Imagery is an example of this. It's a system where predetermined images are placed into the mind for some particular goal (usually something to do with money). Know that the value in these techniques is determined by your intention. Enlightenment and balance should be the aim. If you're using Guided Imagery to help stimulate creativity, Great. If your underlying intention is Enlightenment; go for it. All others … Beware.

The problem with these approaches to imagery is that the ego is doing all the deciding. The unconscious is seen as some sort of dumb animal that has no opinion of its own and no wisdom to contribute. These ideals are birthed from the western world's disrespect for spirit and the inner dimensions. Yes. The fact that they are using inner work as a tactic at all speaks to the fact that there is some sort of acknowledgement of spiritual concepts. But the goals are drenched in materialism and ego gratification which is the source of most of the problems on the planet.

Your unconscious mind does not always have to be filled with detrimental ideas and destructive ways of thought. It can also bring you a level of protection from dangers ahead or it may deter you from completely destroying your life. The unconscious can also sound alarms in an attempt to notify you of an incorrect course of action that you're taking. You may have an inflation of the ego that erroneously directs you into situations that can destroy your marriage, damage your family like, etc. The unconscious may have very good reasons for disagreeing with your projects or goals.

No matter what your goal, when dealing with the unconscious, listening is better than telling. If you want riches, use Active Imagination to help create a balanced individual. Again, your unconscious can be your greatest ally but you must honor and respect it.

Step 3: Be Ethical at All Times

Ethics is a personal standard of conduct that is in accord with an individual's true inner character. Those who behave ethically make an honest effort to conform their behavior to their values. A departure from ethical responsibility deprives a person of wholeness and inflicts fragmentation onto his life. It is our job, as conscious humane human beings, to inject ethics into all facets of our lives.

When it comes to Active Imagination, ground rules need to be set in order to protect the process from becoming a destructive one. Since the creatures that rise out of the unconscious are often, for all intents and purposes, personifications of the impersonal forces of nature, it is we (our conscious sides) who must bring the ethical and humane elements into Active Imagination. These primordial forces that arise are not concerned with human values of justice, service, protection of the defenseless and fairness. You must inject these values into your inner work.

Let's say that during your work and in your imagination, you find yourself at a pool. It could be in Tahiti, Bora Bora, or in a dingy "resort" hotel. All is going well. Suddenly an elderly person falls into the pool and goes beneath the water. What do you do? What would you do if it were physically happening? Your soul is on the line. It is as much the ego's duty to tend to the well-being of the creatures in the inner world as it is to tend to the well-being of fellow humans in the outside world.

There are three major elements in maintaining the ethical aspect of Active Imagination:

1. You add the ethical element by clinging to the attitudes and conduct that are consistent with your character and your deepest values.
2. Ethical balance requires that we not let one archetype or one part of ourselves take over at the expense of the others. We can't sacrifice our values to pursue one narrow goal that serves one side of us but damages another.
3. We must nurture and preserve the human values that serve human life. You must be consistent and unwavering in your protection of your own truth and ideals.

Turning a blind eye to ethics hurts you, both internally and externally and it can be detrimental to the world at large. Not only destruction results but self-destruction and unhealthy extremes come into play. Hold onto your morality when doing inner work. This way you can avoid fragmentation and continue the journey towards oneness.

Step 4: The Ritual

Whenever you do any form of inner work, and when you've successfully resolved a conflict or found a new insight, you should do something to make it concrete. This is where Ritual comes into play. This step is very important because it helps you to integrate your inner experience into your conscious life. A physical act is required, which will affirm the resolution found during inner work.

By physical act, I don't mean to go out and physically act out the fantasy in a literal way. It means to take the core that you have distilled from it – the meaning, insight or principle and externalize it by doing a physical ritual to integrate it into your practical life.

Here's an example. Let's say that based on your inner work, you have discovered that there is a side of you that longs for creative expression. Prior to Active Imagination, you may have traded this urge for creative self-expression in for a corner office accompanied by a 60 hour work week. It has become apparent that this ignored part of you is wreaking havoc on portions of your life.

You have come out of your inner work session with a new insight. Now you must solidify the work done. A few ideas on ritualizing the experience are taking a Thursday night painting class. This gets the creative juices flowing and it satiates that internal part of you that craves the arts. You can draw before going to bed (at least a few nights per week). You can try your hand at ceramics. It does not really matter what you do as long as you attach some physical act to whatever insight you've received.

Here's another example. Prior to doing your inner work, you had a huge aversion to paying your bills. You detest opening an envelope that contains a demand that you relinquish your hard earned cash. You saw a bill and disgust overtook you. Using Active Imagination, you were able to talk to the adolescent boy within who runs from responsibility. You two have made a deal. You have promised to remain light-hearted and fun loving while the scared adolescent boy within has been convinced that paying bills on time provides the opportunity to have even more fun.

You can solidify the end of the conflict by making a commitment to answer your phone within the first ring for all calls from 800 numbers. You know that those calls from 800 numbers are usually calls from bill collectors "attempting to collect on a debt". You commit to the ritual of answering the phone on the first ring.

Whatever your ritual is, it does not have to be elaborate. It can be subtle. Just be very careful not to act out the events of your inner work in real life.

It is suggested that you not use images of people you know in Active Imagination. You run a greater risk of mistaking the inner world for the outer world and confusing states of reality. This can cause you to act inappropriately to the people around you. The best practice is to pause and change the image, if you notice that some form of you has taken on the look of someone from your waking life.

CHAPTER 4:

Sigil Magic – Impressing Upon the Subconscious Mind

Symbols – the Language of the Subconscious

The best way to use your subconscious mind is to use it at a level that you are **not** consciously aware of (which can be tricky). This equates to creating, subconsciously, at the same time that your conscious mind is away doing other things. You do not necessarily want or need your conscious mind to interact with your subconscious creations. Actually, it can be a hindrance.

Subconscious creation happens all the time. You can be subconsciously creating things while you are consciously washing the dishes, doing laundry, cleaning a toilet, whatever and you're conscious mind is not even aware of what is happening. When your conscious mind does not interfere with the subconscious creation of things, creation happens much more quickly, efficiently and thoroughly.

The key to imprinting onto the subconscious lies in the use of symbols. Whether the symbol is a drawing, a tattoo, a hand gesture, a mantra or a dance even, any symbol can act as a gateway to the most powerful part of your mind.

Just as the saying goes, a picture is worth a thousand words so magical symbols can be used to convey a multi-layered message or command. The use of symbols to convey the desire or will is generally referred to as sigil magic.

What is a Sigil?

A sigil is a way of programming your subconscious mind by using an image, etc. to represent your desire. Sigil Magic is a way of taking letters and morphing them into a symbol where the meaning is only known by the subconscious but oblivious to the conscious mind.

A sigil is composed of letters (the language of the conscious mind) formed into symbols (the language of the subconscious mind). This is where the magic happens, between the two realms; between the realm of the conscious mind and the realm of the subconscious mind. Sigils connect the realms by creating a bridge between "concrete" everyday reality (that we perceive with our two eyes) and the unmanifested reality of the "yet to be created".

Much of the power of the sigil lies in your ability to forget your desire. The want must be given to the realm of the unconscious and then not consciously thought of again. If your intention happens to appear in the forefront of your mind, no worries … just don't dwell on it. Let it float away - back into the depths of the unconscious mind. The goal is to tap into the subconscious mind without your conscious mind being aware of it.

You start off by deciding what you want. Now this is not a flimsy step. Deep thought should be given, as you will be held hostage by your true thoughts and beliefs, and not your whimsical fantasies about what you hope you believe. Be very clear about your intention and be sure that it resonates with who you are and your belief system. If these prerequisites are not satisfied, you will fail before you even begin.

Next, you write the well-thought out desire/statement on a sheet of paper. Your statement should be written in **ALL CAPITAL LETTERS** and in the **present tense**. This is so important; *it deserves to be repeated*. **Your statement needs to be written in the present tense.** If you put your statement into the future by using future tense (for instance, "I will"), you will be putting that desire out of your reach. So, it's best to start your statement with "I am", I have", "I possess", etc.

You then take this phrase and create an artistic drawing using the letters in the statement. After you create the sigil, you'll be injecting energy into it (to give it juice). You can do this through meditation, deep concentration, breathing techniques, ritual dance, etc. You have to be aware, concise and deliberate with every step you take because these steps are being recorded by your subconscious mind, as you do them. Your subconscious mind will hold onto your conscious creation and not let go so be diligent and take it very seriously.

Creating a Sigil

There are several different methods you can use to create a sigil.

For simplicity's sake, we will create a very basic sigil using the first letter of each word in your statement (removing all repeated letters).

Let's take the following statement/desire:
I HAVE OPTIMAL HEALTH AND WELL-BEING

Take the first letter of each word & remove any repeated letters:
I H O A W B

Now, let's get to creating our sigil.

You will need two separate sheets of paper; one sheet for your statement/phrase and the other to draw your sigil on. You'll want separate sheets of paper so that your conscious mind does not make a strong connection between the statement and the sigil. Eventually, you'll want to completely disassociate the two (the statement and its symbol/sigil).

After you draw a letter, cross that letter out and cross out all other instances of that letter (if you haven't already). This will insure that you don't mistakenly repeat a letter as there is no need to use any letter more than once.

I H O A W B

I =

H =

O =

A =

W =

B =

Completed =
Sigil

And here is an example of the end sigil but we are not done.

**Completed Sigil =
with Border**

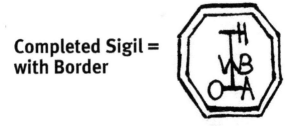

Another important thing about creating your sigil is that you do not want it to be too complex. You can play with the letters, making them overlap, write them upside down, sideways, it's your choice. The more time you spend on it – the more energy you'll be adding to it. The more creative you are with it – the more energy you'll be adding too. Looks don't matter. Simplicity matters. It must resonate with you (so don't rush through any of the steps). Your sigil must be simple enough that you are able to hold it in your imagination and focus on it during ritual.

Remember, it's all about what you think subconsciously. Taking the time to decorate your sigil will make it an even more powerful device by enhancing its effect on your mind, giving it a more magical appeal. The goal is to get your powerhouse (the subconscious mind) aroused so that it will work towards making your desire a reality.

It is very important to have a border around your sigil. The purpose of the border is to contain the energy that you put into the idea contained in the sigil. Remember, the sigil will become an image in your mind that has been injected with spirit power/energy. If you don't put a border around it, the energy that you are directing towards the image in your mind will end up being scattered and unfocused. So, in order to crystalize that energy, you need to put a border around it so that it has a circumference of some type. Your border can be circular, triangular, a polygon ... whatever you like. Remember, the true power resides in you and your beliefs. Through each step of the sigil creation process, use the symbols, thoughts, designs, etc. that are powerful to YOU.

Your sigil will be reminiscent to a puzzle; consciously it will resemble a word puzzle. Your subconscious mind loves puzzles and problems and will be working on this puzzle while you're not consciously aware of it. In fact, after you use your sigil, during a meditation or in a concentration or a raising energy session, your subconscious mind, as you go consciously about your business, is still going to be working on this at a different level and trying to decode which sigil this is.

To make this truly work for you, you should make between 4 and 5 different sigils at the same time. These different sigils should encompass different things that you want to have manifested in your life. The core reasoning behind this is in the forgetting. For success with this you'll need to disassociate your statement from the symbol. Making multiple sigils helps you to disassociate more easily, if from only the sheer number of sigils and statements.

The sigils and the statements should be disassociated then forgotten. Let it slip away into your unconscious, each time you even think the thought will pop-up ... shut it down. Once every week or two you may want to pull your sigils out and just take a look and dwell on them for a moment. Breathe deeply and calm your being then peruse your sigils. You should not remember, yet you will remember (wink, wink).

Sigil magic works best when the subconscious mind is left alone to do its work. If you don't forget the desire/intention, it's like you've planted a seed, but keep running back to it every day to dig it up to see how much it's grown.

This helps to thwart a very real problem associated with sigil magic called Lust of Result. The problem with lusting for the result to happen is that you'll make it impossible for the conscious mind to forget thereby halting the work of your subconscious. You're going to find out that if you make some of your sigils similar, with just slight differences, you're consciously not going to remember which one is which.

Now you might remember the different statements you had written but you don't consciously know which sigil is the one that corresponds with that statement. Consciously, you have just blocked off your conscious mind. Your subconscious mind remembers every minute detail of every second of your day so the sigils are still within its access. Even if it didn't, your subconscious mind will still sit there and try to decode it until it figures out which one it is.

Energizing Your Magical Sigil

Now you have a mind tool. But we're not done yet. Now, we need to super-charge the sigil to make it even more powerful. We do this by adding energy to it. As your subconscious mind thinks about it, and as you conjure life-force energy, that energy will eventually condense in such a way that it will manifest in your life.

The best way to gain access to the subconscious mind is by using what is known as sleight of mind techniques; which focus on modifying consciousness. This means that the conscious mind can be gradually silenced or it can be raised to a higher level/frequency allowing the magical part of the mind to be contacted and directed. You should become familiar with these techniques as there are a multitude of benefits. These sleight of mind techniques are usually grouped into two categories – Silencing Methods and Excitatory Methods.

Silencing methods are aimed at reducing sensory stimulus. These would include meditation and breathing techniques where you would consciously raise your energy by focusing on the slow flow of your breathing while concentrating on the sigil. The greater your concentration, the more power you are pouring into your sigil.

Hopefully, you have been using exercise techniques meant to strengthen concentration (candle meditations for example). Now you'll be able to use these skills with your sigil.

Sit. Clear your mind of all conscious thoughts and just look at the sigil. While you're doing this, think about raising your energy. Actually, imagine it raising. You may want to focus on your breathing too, maintaining an even slow flow. Focus on the sigil. Direct all your energy toward the sigil. Concentrate on the sigil while also being aware of your breathing. The more energy you focus onto it, the quicker your desire will manifest.

The other category of sleight of mind technique has to do with exciting your system to modify your consciousness. Sex magic would fall into this category along with sacred dancing or whirling (to the point of exhaustion). Visualization is extremely beneficial here. For instance, you can close your eyes and envision all the cells in your body vibrating at an extremely fast rate. Or imagine yourself floating in the air above the city or trees or the ocean. Then start spinning. Not literally but in your mind's eye. These excitatory techniques can be fun to do and they're extremely powerful. The goal is to go into trance, to lose yourself in the moment; to shut down your conscious mind to access your subconscious. Music (especially drumming) can bring people to trance. Success here depends on your ability to go into trance as sort of an invitation sent to your subconscious mind.

Even though there is an apparent difference between silencing (the conscious mind) techniques and excitatory techniques both methods imprint the subconscious mind with a desired intention or release a specific suppressed component of the personality to be controlled or invested with energy.

There are many other ways to raise energy. Consider reviewing the section on sexualizing your brain and sex magic. You can combine advanced techniques and mold them into what you need them to be.

After you've created your sigil, injected it with energy and made sure that it is impressed on your subconscious, you'll then want to continue to the last step in the process. You must destroy it. By destroying your sigil, you guarantee that it will be forgotten. Destroy it within a ritual to make it even more powerful to your subconscious mind. Of course, there are unlimited ways to do this. You can burn it. You can rip it up and scatter it to the four winds. You can throw it into a river or you can bury it. Let your imagination be your guide here.

Know that you don't necessarily need to destroy the sigils. As long as you forget, any variation is fine. At the minimum, you should put your sigils away for several weeks then pull them out again. Peruse them slowly to regenerate or reinvigorate the image in your mind.

Sigil Variations

Nothing is written in stone. All is changeable. It is all up to you. Just make sure that all you do resonates with who you are. Let me offer an example. There are those that like body art or tattoos. You can even create a sigil and take it to your local tattoo parlor to have it etched into your skin. Yes, ritualize the whole experience but you will not be destroying your body part. In a case like this, the sigil won't be destroyed. As long as you are forgetting, it is alright.

The choices are yours.

Know that there are different ways of creating sigils. We've used the simplest form for the above example but you should use any variation that resonates with you.

The two additional methods I'll be mentioning differ only in how the letters of the statement are treated/used. All else remains the same (if you'd like them too).

- In one method, all repeated letters are removed.

  Our Statement/Desire: I HAVE OPTIMAL HEALTH AND WELL-BEING
  w/ Repeated Letters Removed: I H A V E O P T M L H N D W B G

- In another method, the vowels are removed along with all repeated letters.

  Our Statement/Desire: I HAVE OPTIMAL HEALTH AND WELL-BEING
  w/ Repeated Letters Removed: I H V P T M L H N D W B G

More Variations:

A tattoo can serve as a sigil. A drawing or painting can serve as a sigil. A hand signal can serve as a sigil. You can even make a sigil out of sound. How you ask? You still want to decide on your intention/desire and write it out as a statement. Take this statement and spell it out phonetically (the way that it sounds). Delete all repeated letters then scramble and rearrange the letters to create a mantra.

Statement or desire: I HAVE OPTIMAL HEALTH AND WELL-BEING
Spell the sentence phonetically: I HAV OPTIMAL HELTH AND WELBEANG
Delete all repeated letters: I H A V O P T M L E N D W B G
Scramble and rearrange the letters to form a mantra: TAL HOV WIPGD NEBM

You'll need to practice with your mantra. Practice until the phrase rolls off your tongue. You'll still want to inject it with energy but your mantra will not have to be destroyed. You can use it in ritual or impress the mantra into subconscious and repeat it mentally.

CONGRATULATIONS!
You now have ways to overcome your conscious mind and tap directly into your subconscious.
You are becoming a co-creator.

CHAPTER 5:

Brainwave Entrainment/Mental Programming Techniques

Change Your Brainwave State - Change Your Life

The human brain is made up of billions of brain cells called neurons, which use electricity to communicate with one another. This combination of millions of neurons sending signals at once produces an enormous amount of electrical activity in the brain, which can be detected using sensitive medical equipment (such as an EEG which measures the electrical levels over areas of the scalp.) The culmination of electrical activity in the brain is commonly known as a brainwave pattern, because of its steady, "wave-like" nature. Brainwaves are graphically represented in the outputs of EEG machines in hospitals and specialist neuro-clinics as wiggly or zigzag lines.

With the discovery of brainwaves came the discovery that electrical activity in the brain will change depending on what the person is doing. For instance, the brainwaves of a sleeping person are vastly different than the brainwaves of someone wide awake. Over the years, more sensitive equipment has brought us closer to figuring out exactly what brainwaves represent and with that, what they mean about a person's health and state of mind.

Nature, wind, crickets, rain, horns – you've heard these beautiful sounds before but not only in the great outdoors. You've probably also heard them through stereo speakers. The CD's with the ocean sounds, the whale calls, and the night sounds (as if you were in a jungle).....very relaxing. You may have seen these types of CD's promoted at metaphysical bookstores, at your local Barnes and Noble's, online, etc. They are said to be able to put you into a relaxed state, relieve stress, heal, cure addictions, etc. They say that these soothing sounds invoke change in your life.

These sounds are more than just bells, nature sounds and soothing music. They also contain technology that has been scientifically proven effective in changing the state of the human mind. This sound technology is being used by psychologist, hypnotherapists and tons of people who wish to have or promote mental and physical well-being.

What is Brainwave Entrainment?

Just as the name suggests, Brainwave Entrainment has to do with training the brain. When we refer to brainwaves, we are referring to the electrical activity in the brain. Brainwave Entrainment refers to the process of stimulating the brain's electrical response using powerful rhythmic sound or light patterns.

A drum beat would even be considered a rhythmic stimulus. The drum is beatin and the rhythm is reproduced in the brain in the form of electrical impulses. If the rhythm is consistent, it can start to resemble the natural internal rhythms of the brain (called brainwaves). When this happens, the brain responds by synchronizing its own electric cycles to the same rhythm. This synchronizing is related to mental states allowing you to enter the gateway to better concentration, meditation, creativity, changing behaviors, and more... Experts attribute this synchronization to a process called the Frequency Following Response (or FFR).

Here is an example of an FFR procedure:

An awake person, who is most likely operating in the Beta brainwave state, would eventually find him/herself totally relaxed and drowsy after a few minutes of listening to tones that correspond to the Alpha brainwave state. Thus, brainwave entrainment is also known as brainwave synchronization.

FFR's have proven to be useful as brainwaves are very much related to mental state. For example, a 4 Hz brainwave is associated with sleep, so a 4 Hz sound pattern would help reproduce the sleep state in your brain. The same concept can be applied to other mental states, including concentration and creativity.

If you listen closely to a brain entrainment session, you will hear short rapid pulses of sound. Background sounds and noise (i.e. rain or a waterfall) are normally embedded into the sound to provide a more relaxing or natural experience. As the session progresses, the frequency rate of these pulses is slowly increased or decreased, thereby changing the brainwave pattern and guiding the mind through various mental states.

Brainwave Entrainment has been used to help with:

• *Relaxation*	• *Intuition and personal insight*
• *Motivation*	• *Focus and attention*
• *Concentration*	• *Problem-solving*
• *Creativity*	• *Promoting long-term mental growth*
• *Memory*	• *Aiding in emotional well-being*
• *Deeper self-awareness*	• *Clarity*
• *Learning*	• *Stress*
• *Behavior Modification*	• *Pain*
• *Energy and vitality*	• *ADD/ADHD*
• *Inspiration*	• *And much, much more*

Mental states are typically described based on the dominant frequency even though your brain is emitting all or most of the different types of brainwaves at any particular moment. You can tell a lot about a person by observing their brainwave patterns. For example, an anxious person will tend to produce a surplus of high Beta waves while people with ADHD/ADD will tend to produce a surplus of slower Alpha/Theta brainwaves.

Here is a table showing the known brainwave types and their associated mental states:

Wave	Frequency	Mental State
Beta	12hz - 38hz	Wide awake, alert mental state. This is generally the mental state most people are in during the day and most of their waking lives. Using self-programming techniques at this level is not very effective, since the mind is not receptive. However, stimulating Beta waves directly can have a huge impact on intelligence, attention, mood, emotional stability and more. Stimulating this can result in relaxation, focus and improved attention. Generally good things to increase. • Beta 1 (15 - 20 Hz) - Can increase mental abilities, IQ, focus • Beta 2 (20 - 38Hz) - Highly alert, but also anxious
Alpha	8hz - 12hz	Awake but deeply relaxed and not processing any information. The brain almost immediately starts producing lots of Alpha upon eyes closed relaxation. This is the mental state you are in early in the morning or while daydreaming. This state enhances the vividness of visualization techniques, and also makes the mind more receptive to suggestion.
Theta	3hz - 8hz	Light sleep or extreme relaxation. Theta is also known as the hyper-suggestive state, where mental programming using recorded affirmations is most effective. • Theta 1 - (3 - 5 Hz) If *suppressed*, can improve concentration, ability to focus attention • Theta 2 - (5 - 8 Hz) Very relaxed and dreamful sleep, good for mental programming
Delta	0.2hz - 3hz	Deep, dreamless sleep. Delta is the slowest band of brainwaves. When your dominant brainwave is Delta, your body is in healing mode. Under most circumstances, you do not dream in this state and are completely unconscious. Entrainment of the brain at this level is difficult. 2 Hz and below is technically not fast enough to produce entrainment, in its strictest sense, and would be seen on an EEG as simple cortical evoked potentials. However, it is theorized that Delta has specific effects on the limbic system, the amygdala and hypothalamus in particular, which operate at delta frequencies. The limbic system affects emotions and the control of autonomic functions. Delta frequencies appear to "sooth" these neural structures and can be very effective reducing migraines, fibromyalgia, chronic pain and blood pressure. Although Delta is generally not as good as Alpha or Theta for meditation, people have found success using Delta for this purpose along with relaxation and, of course, sleep.

Researchers have "discovered" (although known by the ancients) that not only are brainwaves a representation of mental state, but they can be stimulated to transform a person's state, and even help treat a ton of mental disorders. It's also been reported that lucid dreaming and ultra-realistic imagination can also be stimulated (as we step into the world of the psychedelic).

In brief, the 4 Normal Brainwave States are:

1. **Beta state** (13 – 40 cps/Hz): This is the state of mind that we're in during most of the day when we are awake and in action.
2. **Alpha state** (8 – 13 cps/Hz): This occurs when you begin to relax physically and mentally, including the levels where you drift down to very relaxed states like that which happens during meditation, light trance, daydreaming/fantasizing.
3. **Theta state** (4 – 8 cps/Hz): A person is within this level beginning at the border between drowsiness and sleep, down to deep sleep. Experts claim that this is the portal to our subconscious minds where the brain is most receptive to suggestion.
4. **Delta state** (0.5 – 4 cps/Hz): The deepest level of mind, occurring during deep sleep. This is where the body heals itself and produces hormones (such as for growth and anti-aging).

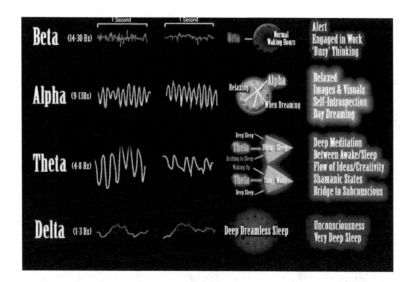

At any particular moment, there are several different frequencies produced by the brain, as seen through an EEG machine. The current state of the brain, however, is determined by the most dominant frequency in the EEG pattern, or the frequency with the highest amplitude.

Above Beta, there are other not-so-common levels such as Gamma and High Gamma.

The "CPS" you see above stands for 'Cycles Per Second' and is a unit also commonly called 'Hertz'. A propeller that rotates 200 times every second is said to have 200 rpm (rotation per second) or 200 cps. A light source flashing 20 times per second is flashing at 20 Hertz.

There are various brainwave entrainment products that target these states and promote certain benefits ranging from stronger intuition and increased creativity to better concentration and recovery from addiction.

Audio/Aural Based Entrainment:

Isochronic Tones are the most effective of all Aural/Audio Entrainment techniques. Isochronic Tones are evenly spaced tone-based pulses that simply turn on and off at a specified rate per second.

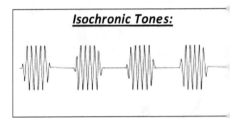

Isochronic Tones:

Because the tones turn off so quickly, they produce extremely strong responses in the brain, which lead to most effective possible brainwave stimulation. Unlike the below entrainment types, Isochronic Tones consist of just one beat/pulse that turns on and off very quickly. A drum beat of 10 beats per second is an isochronic beat. Headphones are NOT required when using this method.

Binaural Beats are created when two waveforms are so close together that they add and subtract enough from each other to be perceived as a pulse, or beat, which can then be used to entrain the brain

Binaural Beats:

(rhythmic stimulus). The frequency of the beats is the same as the difference between the pitches of the 2 tones. For example, if 2 tones, one with a pitch of 200 Hz and the other using 210 Hz, are played at the same time, a pulsating rhythm of 10Hz will result, (the difference between the two). Binaural beats are made of two slightly different tones; one which plays in the left ear
(i.e. 200 Hz) and the other which plays in the right ear (i.e. 210 Hz) so that both ears are technically hearing a different tone.

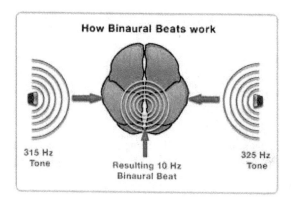

One advantage to using this technique is that in order for the brain to actually create binaural beats, it must use both hemispheres of the brain (right and left), which results in what is called "hemispheric synchronization". Hemispheric Synchronization is when the brainwave pattern of the left and right brain hemispheres becomes similar.

Each ear hears a different tone – the brain produces the pulse/beat – the pulse rate is the numerical difference between the hertz in the tones.

One disadvantage is that Binaural Beats are limited by the limits of the brain's "sound mixing" mechanisms. The pulse produced is so low (less than that of a whisper), that headphones are required. Surround sound stereo systems or people-sized speakers will not help. Headphones are necessary.

Monaural Beats differ from Binaural Beats because they consist of one tone repeated over and over again so that the beat is produced outside of the brain; instead of inside the brain (like Binaural Beats).

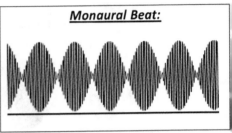

Monaural Beat:

With one tone pulsing on and off in a specific pattern, it is easy to produce the effect you're looking for quickly. Headphones are optional but recommended.

Binaural Beat Generation:

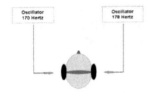

Monaural Beat Generation:

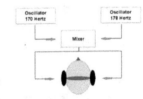

Any pulse of sound can entrain the brain, so it is not limited to just tones. White Noise and even Sound Files can be modulated (or filtered) to provide pulses and other forms of modulation which entrain the brain.

Photic/Light Based Entrainment:

Photic Stimulation involves entraining the brain through the eyes by delivering rhythmic pulses of light at a frequency corresponding to the desired brainwave. Flashing screens, strobe lights, or LED eye-sets are used to produce the same result on the brain as with audio entrainment techniques. Photic Stimulation can be used on its own or in conjunction with audio-based entrainment, like tone pulses.

People have been using light to affect the brain almost as long as they have been using drums to enter into altered states of consciousness. Ptolemy (a Greek astronomer who lived in 1st century Egypt) noted that when looking at the sun through the spokes of a spinning wheel, a feeling of euphoria would take over. Shamans would have their subjects walk single-file past a fire, obscuring the light in a rhythmic fashion. In WWII, many people noticed that those who monitored the radar frequently entered altered mental states because of the rhythmic pulses of light coming from the screen.

Because of modern technology, vivid movies are created using CG effects which can also change brainwave frequency. This is why there is sometimes a warning that appears prior to the start of many movies with high CG effects that caution people with certain conditions (such as epilepsy) that they could be adversely affected.

In fact, strobe lights were first used to alter the minds of the audience. Now they are just a stage effect, but when they first came out they were there for the specific reason of lulling the audience into a certain brain frequency.

Because the input from light stimulation comes through the eyes, it has many distinct differences from other entrainment methods.

First and foremost, because of the immense size of the primary visual cortex it (the visual cortex) can affect surrounding brain areas and cause photic induced seizures in those prone to seizures (such as epileptics), especially when red LED lights are used alone, or when the lights are set too bright. This is one of the reasons it is so important to customize your brain entrainment light session to a comfortable level.

If you are prone to seizures you should *not* use screen flashing or LED eyesets.

One major advantage of photic/light stimulation is that it's been shown to vastly increase blood circulation in the brain (even at very low frequency rates). There are said to be some special advantages in treating PMS, headaches and brain damage.

How Do I Use Photic Stimulation?

To use photic stimulation you need to either use screen flashing (in a dimly lit room) or LED eyesets. In both cases your eyes must be closed.

Yes, you read it correctly: **your eyes must be closed**. Light stimulation relies on the thinness of the eyelids which allows light to pass through.

Color:
If you use screen flashing or LED glasses that allow you to customize the color combinations, you will be able to generate some special effects. Below is a list of colors and their associated effects.

Red - Red is good for energy, body building, and adrenaline and is also the universal color of sexual attraction. Unfortunately, it is not very relaxing and tends to produce a "fight or flight" response, or heightened anxiety, in beginners. Red should generally not be used alone.

Brown - Brown helps reduce depression, irritability, and chronic fatigue and it also helps with migraine headaches, the immune system and mood regulation.

Orange - Good for increasing appetite and slowing the rate of blood flow.

Yellow - Yellow can be used for creativity and insight, but may not be very relaxing.

Green - A peaceful, soothing color, much like blue. Green has also been known to reduce allergic reaction to foods and MSG.

Blue - A soothing color, great for relaxation. It has also been known to increase metabolism, promote growth and cause the brain to release eleven different neurotransmitters. Pulse rate will slow and breathing will slow. Use blue for stress and anxiety relief, or general relaxation.

Indigo - Good for reducing pain and releasing endorphins.

Violet - The so-called "spiritual" color. Violent tends to bring out the spiritual side of people in all cultures. It has also been reported to help reduce hunger and irritability.

White (or a combination of colors) - Good for visualization, since more (or all) of the color spectrum is represented.

CHAPTER 6:

Pre-Programming Using Anchors and Triggers

Anchoring is a neuro-linguistic programming term describing the process by which brainwave state change become associated with (anchored to) some stimulus, in such a way that perception of the stimulus (the anchor) leads by reflex to the reoccurrence of the anchored response. In simpler terms, an anchor is when your state changes in response to a trigger (stimulus). The stimulus can be neutral and even out of your conscious awareness. The response can be either positive or negative and it's capable of being formed and reinforced by repeated stimuli; making it similar to conditioning or programming.

An example of an anchor is when you're driving and hear sirens. You may not know whether it's a police car, a fire truck or an ambulance but your automatic response is to pull the car over to the side. The siren, known as the stimulus, triggered your response to slow down and pull the car over. Anchors can be related to a positive response or a negative response.

A few examples of positive anchors and triggers are:

- An old love song re-awakens a romantic mood.

- Picking up a childhood toy takes you back to Christmas 35 years ago and the feelings associated with it.
- A gentle touch by a loved one gets your juices flowing and raises excitement.
- Your mother angrily says your full name and you think of a belt across your behind.
- Even seeing a red traffic light automatically makes some drivers stop (or speed up) without conscious thought.

A few examples of not so positive anchors and triggers are:

- You hear a police siren and start running. It takes you back to your younger track star days, hopping fences.
- You smell McDonald's fries and your stomach overrides your brain and you go buy some. (Those things will kill ya).
- Being alone and needing comfort, you head for the fridge for some good ole comfort food.
- Lays Potato Chips – you can't eat just one (get some exercise).
- A person that has been traumatized may hear a sudden noise and be taken mentally back to a terrifying experience.

Understandably, some people struggle with triggers/anchors because they feel they are not in control. Anchors are the domain of the unconscious/subconscious mind. In other words, they aren't conscious thoughts, so you don't think "I can hear an ambulance siren so there must be an ambulance around". You don't have that kind of time. You just instantly know what the sound is so you just pull over. You don't have to give it any thought whatsoever.

Anchoring can be used to facilitate state management. When used this way, an anchor is created by a deliberately chosen stimulus and then linked by repetition to the desired state in order to provide easy access to that state, at will. Unbeknownst to most, we are creating anchors most of the day.

When I go jogging (as if), I put on the Eye of the Tiger song from the Rocky III movie. I hear those guitars and I'm psyched within about 10 seconds. I've repeated the process so much that I automatically get a boost of energy. My heart rate increases. My breathing gets faster; all without my conscious knowledge. This is an example of repetition anchoring a feeling and physical response which eventually becomes automatic when the stimuli is presented.

Marketing companies use anchors all-the-time. The Kia car commercial with the hamsters comes to mind. They use one of my childhood favorite songs in the commercial (This or That by Black Sheep). Each time I hear that EVIL song, I think of hamsters in a car in urban wear. My favorite part of the song comes on and instead of me getting nostalgic over the memories of partying in the 90's, I only see (in my head) hamsters bopping their heads and hamsters dancing in the street. UGH.

Now that you're becoming familiar with Anchors and Triggers, let's discuss how you can create them and use them for your benefit. There are 3 major facets to creating anchors and they are:

1. Intensity – Your anchor must be created while at your optimal emotional intensity. Get yourself to the desired state by imagining what it would be like to be in that state or by remembering a time when you were in that state. If you want to feel empowered or motivated, get yourself to that state mentally but for best results, get your body involved; get the blood flowing….shadow box, whatever you need to do to bring intensity to anchoring.

2. Repetition – when dealing with programming, repetition is also referred to as "stacking the anchor". The more times you set the trigger/stimulus while feeling the extreme of the desired emotion the more that trigger will become associated with or anchored to that emotion and the more effective it will be for you.

3. Uniqueness – To assure that your trigger is not fired off at the wrong time, it is very important that your trigger/anchor be unique.

This is how the plan comes together.

1) First, think of an emotion you would like to anchor. Total self-confidence maybe? Or the feeling of being enthusiastic perhaps?

2) Think of an anchor that you would like to use. Uniqueness is the key. For example, you can cross your pinky finger and your ring finger on your right hand. Or you can tug on your left eyebrow. Or you can tuck your thumb into your fist. It doesn't really matter what the trigger is as long as it is unique.

3) Recall or imagine the emotion you wish to anchor and get yourself as emotionally keyed in as possible.

4) Engage your trigger. Once you've done that, release your trigger and get yourself back to your normal state.

5) Repeat as much as you like, the more you do it, the more powerful the anchor becomes.

CHAPTER 7:

Real-Time Mental Programming

In this chapter we will discuss some techniques that you can use to quickly affect the way your mind is functioning. These techniques are not as powerful as the previously mentioned PRE-programming tools but the huge advantage is that they can be used at any time.

Here are some techniques that can be used to quickly bypass mental filters and affect your brain at its core.

Guidelines and Tips:

1. Relax – Relaxation is actually a requirement for all types of mental programming. A distracted or agitated mind is operating above the alpha brainwave state and therefore is not receptive to reprogramming. Breathe deeply from your abdomen – Relax Your Shoulders – Relax Your Legs – Relax Your Whole Being.

Relaxation Tips:

- Check for tension: If you let tension win, you may as well go do something else; you're done. Forget about altering your brainwaves because it just won't happen if you're tense. Help tension dissolve by slowly scanning your body. Spend 5 to 15 seconds on each body part starting with your toes. Then go up to your calf muscles, then thighs on up to the top of your head. Instruct the tension to disappear.

- Keep Your Eyes Closed: As previously mentioned, closing your eyes will automatically place your brain into alpha state. Closed eyes eliminate about 80 percent of external stimulation so this is key.

- Keep Your Eyes Pointing Upwards: It's been scientifically proven that people naturally look up when trying to solve a math problem or trying to remember something visual. When you look up, the visual part of your brain is stimulated and massive amounts of Alpha brainwaves are produced. So when your eyes are closed, move them slightly upwards. Comfort is paramount so if you feel any eye strain, move your eyes down to a comfortable position.

- Count Down to Relaxation: You've seen hypnotists do it. When they are taking a person "under", notice how their speech is very soft and rhythmic. And it goes a little something like this: *"Ten.. I am relaxing more and more with every number I count. Nine... I am continuing to relax with every number I count. Eight... at the count of zero I am completely relaxed. Seven... my mind and body are completely relaxed at the count of 0......" and so on.* Mothers of children are known to sing a lullaby or two. The name itself alludes to a lulling. Lulling to sleep.

Mom sings softly and slowly and soon the little boy or girl is drooling. She has just brought her baby down to low alpha state.

- Breathe Through Your Abdominals: Your breathing is directly related to your brainwave state. Slow, deep, even breathing will help you to quickly relax. Breathing from your chest will give you the opposite effect of what you actually want; as chest breathing is associated with the Fight or Flight response. Abdominal breathing will relax and rejuvenate you. You'll know that you are breathing correctly, when your belly expands and contracts while your chest stays relatively unmoved.
- Visualize – see next section please.

2. Use Visualization and Imagination – NOT Willpower – Remember that willpower is meant to fail when going against programming. Use your willpower to make yourself visualize. Visualization is the creative use of the imagination for self-improvement. Visualization is vital for effective mental programming and is a powerful tactic to use in conjunction with affirmations and auto-suggestion. Use your imagination and picture (in your mind's eye) what you want to happen. Always visualize in the third person as if you're watching yourself do something. With some practice, your imagination will team up with your willpower in a powerful partnership focused on making your life the best it can be.

There is a downside to visualization. Actually, it's more like a gift and a curse. The downside to visualization is that it often causes a self-fulfilling prophecy motif. It can be your worst enemy wrecking total and complete havoc on your life if you don't realize the power involved. Many people have incorrectly thought that they possessed some type of psychic foresight not realizing that they've only imagined something happening and their subconscious actually made it happen. Have you ever got into your car and had the idea of an accident barge into your thoughts? Then what happened. You got into an accident. Or in those movies that take place in the Himalayas. One mountain climber tells a novice "Whatever you do, don't – look – down." But what happens, the new jack looks down and is now paralyzed by fear. The subconscious mind is powerful beyond measure and you can use it to your advantage.

Visualization Tips:

- Make your visualizations as real as possible. Add color and sound; see all sides of objects and practice. The more you practice, the more vivid your imaginings will be.
- Do all work in the 3rd person. View your visualizations as if you're watching a movie. For some reason (not completely known by modern science), visualizing from another's point of view, multiplies its power.
- You do not have to actually be in the scene. You can imagine a hamburger then imagine clogged arteries if you want to eat more healthy foods. Imagining clogged arteries will nauseate you and stop any cravings for burgers.
- Use Objects to impress upon your subconscious. If you have a job with a boss that has trouble listing to suggestions, you can imagine a florescent light bulb smashing over your bosses head. Now they see the light. (Remember your visualizations not only affect you but others too.)
- Feel everything within the scene. Smell the smells. Feel the related emotions. If you are visualizing yourself

winning a marathon, make yourself feel the "thrill of victory". If you're visualizing yourself giving a moving speech, make yourself feel confidence and the love from the crowd.

- Increase the brightness and color of any scenes that give you your desired feeling. Make the colors very vivid and give it intense lighting.

- Ignore what you don't want. Give no attention to anything that is not associated with the desired feeling or outcome. Focus on one issue or goal at a time and stay focused.

- Desensitize yourself to any unpleasant scenes or memories that pop-up. You can do this by making the scene hazy, switching the scene from color to black and white, etc. For example, if imaging a public speaking engagement, imagine that everyone in the crowd is naked. Oh, you've heard that one before? It works.

3. Realize Your Authority – Your mind is a powerhouse. Your mind is the motivator and generator of all your movements. The mind commands, the body obeys without question. The mind is in complete control. If you can effectively control your mind, you will become the supreme ruler over your life. Once you realize this, you will understand that you have all the authority. The next time you have a pain, close your eyes, breathe deeply, and know that you have the power then gently will the pain away.

4. Un-focus Your Eyes – We mentioned earlier that closing your eyes automatically eases your mind into alpha state. Un-focusing your eyes also has the effect of stimulating alpha waves within your brain. Un-focusing can also help you desensitize yourself from what you're seeing which is very

helpful during potentially traumatic events. You can also use this to accelerate learning or to gain a different outlook on a situation. The next time you are studying something, take in the info first with your eyes open, and then repeat the information to yourself with your eyes closed. You'll notice that the feeling is different. You'll see that you'll have a fuller understanding with added clarity.

5. Pre-Programming for Real-Time Situations – This involves using an Anchor as a trigger or stimulus that retrieves a desired emotional or brainwave state. For further information on pre-programming for real-time situations, see the previous chapter entitled Pre-Programming Using Anchors and Triggers. You'll learn what anchors and triggers are and how this type of pre-programming will help you instantly stimulate the onset of your desired emotion/state.

CHAPTER 8:

Mental Operating System Health & Maintenance

Below are some helpful tips for maintaining the Super-Computer Called Your Mind.

1. Self-Talk and Thought Patterns

   It is extremely important to monitor the words you use on yourself. Although few will admit it, most people talk to themselves on a regular basis. Whether out loud or in their own heads, people converse with themselves often and it's usually not pretty. People spout terrible words about themselves to themselves without understanding that the mind is taking these words as truth. Beware, because even when we are joking, the mind takes our words literally and funnels them to our subconscious.

   Yes. I know that sometimes an embarrassing or painful memory may come to the surface of your mind but phrases like "that was dumb" or "I was such an a**hole" or "you fool" simply will not serve you. Add repetition to the mix and there it goes. You are implanting damaging ideas about yourself into your subconscious.

Like two sides of the same coin, there are also some huge advantages to self-talk. The trick is this. NEVER allow a negative phrase or thought to complete itself. Stop it in its tracks and change it. Most people can catch themselves in the middle of a negative thought and reconstruct it. For example, let's say you recall a painful relationship from your past and you begin to proclaim, "I'm such a doormat...I let people walk all over me" but catch yourself and switch it up. Say, "I'm such a wonderful person and people love to be around me".

Get used to NOT insulting yourself. Get used to empowering yourself. Develop the habit of injecting love and power into your self-talk instead of calling yourself stupid or dumb or a weakling. Begin integrating your speech patterns with your goals. You can say to yourself "I am confident or healthy or lovable or a dynamo". After a very short time, you'll notice that your "negative" thoughts will evoke images of you as you want to be.

2. Meditation

Heck no, I'm not going into detail on this one. There is so much info available online on this subject that you'd be reading for months. I suggest you use brainwave entrainment software to have quicker results than conventional meditation techniques. Whether going conventional or modern, decreasing your brainwaves to Alpha and Theta states have extremely helpful effects on the brain; sort of like a brain tune-up. Meditation allows you to traverse your subconscious mind and take delight in mental imagery. You can create whole worlds within the mind, and have fun doing it.

3.   Sleep is a Workshop

What do you think of when you've retired for the day and are drifting off to sleep? Well, most people revisit the happenings of the day whether they want to or not. Many times, worries stream into consciousness making it hard to even get to sleep. It boils down to your subconscious mind entertaining disempowering thoughts as you drop from Beta to Alpha to Theta to Delta.

This is not a healthy situation but it happens every night for most people. Not only is this a waste of your subconscious powerhouse but it's extremely detrimental to allow worries into our sleep routine. We are actually giving power to the worry and fear as they plunge directly into our subconscious mind. We do not want to empower the wrong ideas.

When dozing off, use visualizations and affirmations to communicate your goals to your subconscious. As you sleep, your mind will reinforce your goals and act on them with the power of not just one human mind but the universal mind. Reality will bend to your will.

4.   Develop a Collection of Anchors/Triggers

Review the chapter on Anchors and Triggers then take the time to develop your own personal arsenal. Then you'll have immediate access to relaxation, creativity, heightened learning, whatever mental state you wish to experience. Imagine this. Let's say you won an award for something; think of the pride and happiness that you felt. That too can be anchored for easy access on a future date. Your arsenal of healthy anchors will prove to be helpful and even indispensable.

5.   Reinforce Your Beneficial Mental Programs

You may experience times where the mental programs you've implemented begin to wear off. They may not be as powerful as they once were. This will happen from time to time. For this reason, it's important to review your programs for effectiveness. You may notice that the power has subsided or lost its potency. It's okay. Just take inventory and reinforce when needed.

Final Thoughts:

Not meant for the mundane levels of your simple wants and whims; I hope that this book will serve as your companion as you delve into the deeper levels of your life's purpose(s) and your heart's true desires. Awaken your inner intelligences. Align your ideals. And not only will wealth follow but inner happiness will reign.

Recommended Reading and Software:

Recommended Reading:

Jung, Carl Gustav. Archetypes of the Collective Unconscious
Murphy, Dr. Joseph. The Power of the Subconscious Mind
Miller, Dr. Emmett E. Software For The Mind
Wise, Anna. Awakening The Mind
Jung, Carl Gustav. Jung on Active Imagination
Jung, Carl Gustav. The Portable Jung
Campbell, Joseph. The Hero With a Thousand Faces
Shinn, Florence Scovel. The Collection
Bandler, Richard. Guide to Trance-formation

Recommended Software (w/ Risk Free Trial):

Mind Workstation
BrainIgniter Player
Neuro-Programmer 2 or 3

CPSIA information can be obtained
at www.ICGtesting.com
Printed in the USA
LVHW020504280720
661655LV00014B/1825